For those building something real, and those who are about to.

To the mentors who told me the truth when it would have been easier to say nothing, the employees who showed up and made the business real, and the customers who handed over their trust and kept coming back —

You know who you are. Thank you.

Contents

A NOTE FROM THE TRENCHES

I have no formal business education. No MBA. No fancy business school pedigree.

I've spent time in two very different trenches. Seventeen years in corporate, building teams, fighting for customers, and watching good work get restructured away by decisions made in boardrooms I was never invited into. Then fifteen years as an entrepreneur, building from nothing, making payroll by the skin of my teeth, and eventually creating something rewarding that runs without me.

What I share in these pages comes straight from those trenches — the principles that actually moved the needle for me. The ones that reduced daily stress, improved team performance, protected cash flow, and built real long-term value. They're not theory. They're what worked when the business was on my shoulders and the mental load felt heavy.

Whether you run a service business, a trades operation, a landscaping company, a cleaning service, or anything in between, these principles apply if you depend on people, systems, and customers to generate revenue.

But there's something I want you to understand before you read a single principle.

From the very first day you open your doors, you are building something. The question is whether you're building it intentionally — or just surviving.

Every decision you make as an owner should be filtered through one question: does this make my business more valuable or less valuable? Clean books. Systems that run without you. A brand that belongs to the business — not to your name or your personality. A team that delivers consistent results whether you're in the building or not.

I've seen owners pour years of their lives into something and walk away with far less than it was worth — not because the business wasn't good, but because it wasn't transferable. The finances were tangled. The owner was the brand. The customers had relationships with the person, not the company. None of that is easy to fix at the end. It has to be built right from the beginning.

The ultimate reward for everything you sacrifice — every early morning, every sleepless night, every Friday you spend holding your breath waiting for payroll to clear — is the exit. The day you hand over the keys and walk away with something that genuinely changes your life. That day is worth planning for from the beginning.

Build something someone would want to buy. Everything else flows from that.

If you're a small business owner trying to grow without losing your sanity, or wanting to create something healthy enough that it could one day reward you with a strong exit, I hope these practical ideas save you some of the pain I went through and give you more freedom along the way.

I'm still learning every day. These are simply the lessons I wish someone had handed me earlier in the journey.

Welcome to the trenches.

— Scott Waterman

Service Business Operator and U.S. Army National Guard Veteran

PRINCIPLE 1: Start Smart with Realistic Planning and Capital

Growth is expensive. In service businesses, costs often rise faster than revenue in the first 1–4 years. Most owners underestimate how much capital they actually need — and that gap creates stress, forces bad decisions, and can sink an otherwise good business before it ever gets off the ground.

In the early days of scaling my business, cash flow was a constant source of anxiety. Every Friday morning I'd wake up with a knot in my stomach, hoping deposits would hit the account in time for payroll to clear.

Employees got paid first. That was non-negotiable. I was paid last.

I spent far too much mental energy timing payables, juggling invoices, and refreshing my bank balance just to make sure we wouldn't bottom out. It was exhausting, and it was stealing focus I needed to actually grow the business.

Because I had no established business credit early on, banks weren't helpful when I needed funding. I had to borrow personally to bridge the gaps, which hurt my personal credit through high debt ratios and hard inquiries. In an ideal world, you'd build business credit early and use more sophisticated tools — but that's not always possible when you're just starting out or scaling fast.

One conversation that stuck with me happened early on. One of my first customers pulled me aside and encouraged me to stick with it. He said the hump could easily take five years, but if I kept going it would be worth it. That moment felt like yesterday. It gave me perspective when things felt darkest.

The constant checking eventually became too much. One day I made a deliberate decision to stop obsessively monitoring the balance and focus on the things I could control. I trusted that if I kept doing the right things, the business would eventually get the lift it needed.

Months later, when I finally logged in, I braced myself for the usual pit in my stomach. Instead, I was stunned. The account balance was dramatically higher than I expected — enough to cover three full months of operating expenses, and then some. I was finally over the hump. The fear of bouncing a payroll check disappeared along with the anxiety I felt every time I logged into my account.

Looking back, I'm glad I didn't give up. I've since paid off all that debt and reached a point where work is optional — not someday, now. That experience shaped everything I now believe about capital planning — and it's why this is the first principle in this book.

What Nobody Tells You Before You Start

Most business advice focuses on the exciting parts — the idea, the launch, the growth. Very few people sit you down and say: *"Here's what the first two years actually feel like financially, and here's how to survive them."*

The truth is that service businesses are cash-intensive before they become cash-generative. You're paying for labor, equipment, insurance, and overhead before the revenue fully catches up. If you're not prepared for that gap — mentally and financially — it will break you.

This isn't a reason not to start. It's a reason to start smart.

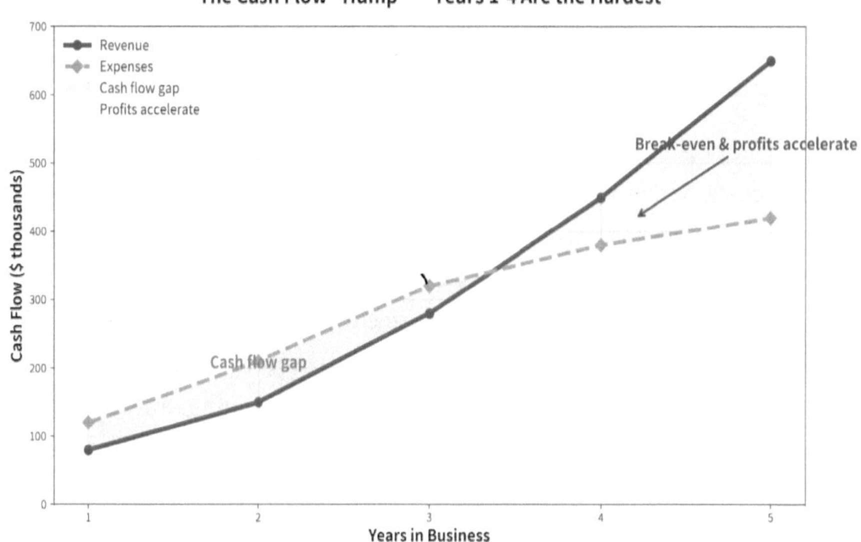

Expenses level off as the business matures — better vendor terms, bulk purchasing, streamlined SOPs, and operational synergies. Revenue keeps growing because the foundation is solid.

Build Business Credit Early — Before You Need It

One of my biggest early mistakes was waiting until I needed financing to think about credit. By then it was too late. Banks want to lend to businesses that don't desperately need the money.

Start building business credit from day one. Open a dedicated business checking account and a business credit card. Pay everything on time. Keep your personal and business finances completely separate — not just for credit purposes, but because commingling finances makes your books a mess and creates problems when you need to show a lender or a buyer a clean picture of the business.

Look into a business line of credit early (ideally while your financials are still strong and you don't urgently need it). A line of credit sitting unused is one of the most valuable things a small business owner can have. It's not debt. It's options.

Know Your Numbers Before You Spend

Before you hire your first employee, sign your first lease, or make any significant investment, build a simple 12 to 18 month cash flow projection. It doesn't need to be complicated. Map out your expected revenue based on realistic (not optimistic) assumptions. Then map out your fixed costs, your variable costs, and any one-time or seasonal expenses.

Run three scenarios: best case, worst case, and most likely. Then plan for somewhere between worst case and most likely. If the math still works, move forward. If it doesn't, adjust before you're committed.

Update that projection every single month. Treat it like a living document. The moment you see a gap forming — revenue softening, an unexpected expense, a slow season approaching — you can take action while you still have runway. Cut non-essential spending, accelerate collections, or line up financing before you're desperate for it.

The owners who survive the early years aren't always the ones with the best ideas. They're the ones who saw the cash flow problem coming and dealt with it before it became a crisis.

Separate Your Finances Completely

This deserves its own moment because so many new owners get it wrong.

Keep your personal and business finances completely separate from day one. Separate bank accounts. Separate credit cards. Separate everything.

Mixing personal and business finances doesn't just create accounting headaches — it obscures the true health of your business, complicates your taxes, and raises red flags with lenders and buyers down the road. If you ever want to sell your business, a clean set of books is one of the most valuable things you can present to a buyer. Commingled finances are one of the first things that kill deals.

Pay yourself a defined salary or draw. Anything beyond that should be a documented distribution — not a random transfer to cover a personal expense. Discipline here early saves enormous pain later.

Protect Payroll Above Everything Else

If you have employees, payroll is sacred. It is the one bill you never miss, never delay, and never compromise on.

Your employees show up and do their jobs trusting that you will hold up your end of the agreement. The moment you break that trust — even once — you risk damaging something that is very hard to repair. Beyond the human cost, missing payroll creates legal exposure that no small business owner can afford.

Build your cash management around payroll first. Everything else gets managed around it.

The Mental Load Is Real — Plan for It

Nobody prepares you for the psychological weight of financial uncertainty when you're running a small business. The sleepless nights, the constant mental math, the anxiety of watching a balance you can't fully control — it's real and it's exhausting.

The best antidote I found wasn't more revenue. It was more visibility. When I knew exactly where I stood financially (when I had a projection I trusted and a buffer I could count on), the anxiety didn't disappear, but it became manageable. I was leading instead of reacting.

A cash buffer of two to three months of operating expenses isn't a luxury. It's the difference between making good decisions and making desperate ones.

Remember the End Game

Every decision you make as a business owner should be filtered through one question: *does this make my business more valuable or less valuable?*

From the very beginning (before you've hired your first employee or signed your first customer), you should be building as if you intend to sell. Not because you have to sell, but because a business built to be sellable is also a business built to run well, scale cleanly, and give you options.

That means clean books. It means systems that don't depend on you personally. It means a brand that belongs to the business — not to your name or your personality. The moment your business becomes inseparable from you as an individual, you've reduced its value to a future buyer. A buyer isn't just purchasing revenue. They're purchasing something they can operate, grow, and eventually sell themselves. If the whole thing falls apart without you in the room, that's not a business — that's a job with overhead.

As someone who has acquired businesses and routes, I've seen firsthand what buyers actually look at. The ones that commanded full price had clean books, documented systems, and customers loyal to the brand. The ones that didn't — the finances were incomplete, the owner was indispensable, and the customer relationships walked out the door with the seller. By the time most owners realize that's a problem, the window to fix it has already closed.

Everything you're building is pointing somewhere. The systems, the team, the clean books, the loyal customers — none of it is just about keeping the lights on. It's about creating something with real value. Something transferable. Whether that means financial freedom at closing or handing the keys to someone in your family, the destination matters. Start building toward it today, not someday. The owner who plans for exit from the beginning builds a fundamentally different business. Start today.

Action Checklist:

- Build a realistic 12 to 18 month cash flow projection before aggressive growth
- Run best case, worst case, and most likely scenarios — plan conservatively
- Open dedicated business banking and credit accounts from day one
- Keep personal and business finances completely separate
- Start building business credit immediately — before you need it
- Secure a business line of credit while your financials are strong
- Aim for a cash buffer of two to three months of operating expenses
- Update your cash flow projection every month without exception
- Protect payroll above all other obligations
- When you see a gap forming, act early — don't wait until you're in crisis
- Pay yourself a defined, consistent amount — document everything beyond that
- Remember: the mental load of financial uncertainty is manageable with visibility and planning

PRINCIPLE 2: Hire for Attitude First — Skills Can Be Taught

Technical skills can be trained. Attitude, reliability, and coachability are much harder to develop — and they make the biggest difference when you're scaling a service business that depends on people showing up and doing the job right every day.

Early on I hired for skills. I needed someone who could do the job. Competence felt like the logical filter. It wasn't.

The people who caused the most problems weren't the ones who needed training. They were the ones who had bad attitudes, called out constantly, or simply didn't care. Skills I could teach. Work ethic I couldn't.

One employee asked to leave early for an emergency haircut. I'm not kidding. Some people will show you their priorities without even realizing it. That moment stuck with me.

After enough of those experiences I changed my approach. I stopped leading with "can they do the job?" and started leading with "are they the kind of person I want representing this business?"

Learning to Let Go

Here's something most business owners won't admit: hiring the right people is only half the battle. The other half is trusting them to do the job.

When you've built something from scratch with your own hands, relinquishing control is genuinely hard. You have standards. You know exactly how things should be done. And early on, nobody does it quite the way you would.

I struggled with this more than I'd like to admit. My instinct was always to step in, correct, and take over. But I eventually realized that micromanaging good people drives them away — and it keeps you trapped in the business instead of working on it.

The shift came when I stopped asking "are they doing it my way?" and started asking "are they getting the right result?" Giving people ownership over their work — with clear expectations and consistent coaching — is what eventually allowed me to step back from daily operations entirely. But it required me to trust the process and trust the people I'd hired.

That trust has to be earned on both sides. Which is exactly why how you hire matters so much.

A Word on Hiring Friends and Family

I've done it. And when it went wrong it cost me more than just an employee.

I'm not saying never do it — sometimes people you know are genuinely the right fit. But go in with your eyes open. The personal relationship makes accountability much harder. When performance conversations become personal, when someone's feelings get hurt, when you have to let someone go — the professional problem becomes a personal one fast.

If you do hire someone you're close to, treat them exactly like any other employee from day one. Same expectations. Same check-ins. Same standards. The moment you make exceptions because of the relationship, you've created a problem you'll have to manage forever.

My advice: exhaust every other option first.

Where to Find Good People

Most newer owners underestimate how close good candidates already are. Some of my best hires came from referrals from existing employees — people who already understood the culture and had something at stake in recommending someone reliable. A simple referral bonus goes a long way.

Beyond that, Indeed and Facebook community groups work well for entry-level service roles. Local community colleges, trade programs, and neighborhood social media groups can surface motivated candidates who are looking for stable, consistent work in their area. Don't overlook people who are underemployed — someone who shows up every day and genuinely wants to do good work is worth more than a polished resume from someone who'll leave the moment something better comes along.

How I Actually Interview

I use a simple behavioral interview format (asking candidates to walk me through real situations they've faced, what they did, and what happened). It cuts through polished answers fast.

For front-line service roles I'd ask things like:

"Tell me about a time you showed up for someone who was counting on you, even when it was inconvenient."

"Tell me about a job where things didn't go as planned. What did you do?"

"Have you ever disagreed with a manager or coworker? How did you handle it?"

You learn more from those answers than from anything on a resume. Listen for accountability, self-awareness, and how they talk about past employers. Someone who blames everyone else for everything that went wrong at their last job will bring that pattern into your business too.

I also throw in a situational question or two — *"What would you do if a customer called upset about something outside your control?"* — to see how they think on their feet.

Setting Clear Expectations from Day One

One of the most common mistakes new owners make is assuming people will figure things out. They won't (at least not the way you want them to).

Before a new hire starts, make sure they have a written job description that outlines exactly what they're responsible for, what good performance looks like, and how they'll be evaluated. It doesn't have to be elaborate. A one-page document that answers "what does success look like in this role?" is enough.

The first week should be structured — who they shadow, what they learn, and when you check in. A simple first-week checklist removes ambiguity and sets the tone that this is a professional operation, even if it's a small one.

The First 90 Days

I built a structured first 90 days into every hire. Both sides get a low-pressure window to honestly evaluate fit — the employee sees if they like the culture, and I see how they handle real expectations. Check-ins at 30, 60, and 90 days keep it honest.

At 30 days I ask: Are they showing up? Are they coachable? Are they fitting in with the team?

At 60 days: Are they improving? Do they need more support or are they running on their own?

At 90 days: Is this a long-term fit?

This structure protects the business legally and practically — documented check-ins create a paper trail if a separation becomes necessary. But more importantly it gives you a natural, low-drama framework to have honest conversations before small problems become big ones.

Watch for Who Has More in Them

The 90 days isn't just about whether someone survives the probation period. It's also your best window to spot who has more in them than the job requires.

The person who asks good questions, notices things without being told, and takes ownership without being pushed — that's someone worth investing in. Watch for the employee who stays a few minutes late to make sure something is done right, or who comes to you with a solution instead of just a problem. Those are signals.

I've promoted from within more than once and it changed my business. People who grow into leadership inside your operation already understand the culture, the customers, and the standards. You don't have to teach them who you are.

Watch for it early. Sometimes the best manager you'll ever have walks in the door applying for an entry-level position.

What If It's Not Working?

This is the part nobody talks about — and it's where most new owners freeze.

If the 90-day check-ins are showing red flags, trust what you're seeing. Document the conversations. Be specific about what isn't meeting expectations and give the person a fair chance to correct it. Most people respond to honest, direct feedback — especially when it's delivered with respect.

If it still isn't working after that, let them go cleanly and professionally. A short, honest conversation is kinder than dragging it out. *"This isn't the right fit for either of us"* is a complete sentence.

The longer you wait to address a bad hire, the more damage they do to your team's morale and your own peace of mind. There's a reason people say "hire slow, fire fast," even if the phrase sounds harsh. The deeper lesson is not to let obvious misalignment linger indefinitely.

Don't Overlook What's Already in Front of You

Some of my best people were already working for me when I needed to fill a bigger role. Promoting from within rewards loyalty, preserves culture, and sends a message to everyone on the team that there's a path forward. Before you post a job externally, ask yourself whether someone already in your operation has earned the opportunity.

In my experience, the best teams aren't built by finding perfect people. They're built by finding the right people and investing in them consistently.

Action Checklist:

- Source candidates through employee referrals first — consider a small referral bonus
- Post on Indeed and local Facebook groups for entry-level service roles
- Be cautious about hiring friends and family — if you do, hold them to the same standards as everyone else
- Prioritize work ethic, coachability, and reliability over technical skills
- Use behavioral questions — *"Tell me about a time when..."*
- Ask for specific examples from past roles, not just hypotheticals
- Include situational questions to see how they think on their feet
- Provide a written job description and first-week checklist before day one
- Set clear performance expectations from the start
- Build a structured 90-day onboarding with check-ins at 30, 60, and 90 days
- Document every check-in conversation
- During the 90 days, watch for employees who show potential for more responsibility
- Address performance issues directly and early — don't let them fester
- Look internally before posting externally
- Work on trusting your team — micromanaging drives good people away

PRINCIPLE 3: Address Growing Pains — From Nimble Bicycle to a Moving Freight Train

When your service business grows, the work never stops. Customers expect service every single day. You can't shut down for a week to retool, regroup, or give the team a breath with any sort of ease. The operation becomes a moving freight train — powerful and full of momentum, but far less agile than it used to be.

Understanding that reality early is one of the most important things a service business owner can do.

From Bicycle to Freight Train

When you start a service business it feels like riding a bicycle. You power it. You steer it. You can stop it instantly, turn on a dime, and pick it up and carry it if you need to. It goes exactly where you point it because it runs entirely on your energy and your decisions.

That's exhilarating. It's also exhausting. But it works — because at that stage, speed and agility are your biggest advantages over larger competitors.

Then something shifts.

You add customers. You hire people. You build processes. The bicycle becomes a freight train — powerful, full of momentum, and capable of serving far more people than you ever could alone. But it no longer stops on a dime. Changing direction requires planning well in advance. And unlike the bicycle, it doesn't run on your energy anymore. It runs on systems, people, and momentum.

Most owners make the mistake of still trying to ride it like a bicycle long after it has become a freight train. They make snap decisions that create downstream chaos. They change direction without warning and watch their team scramble to keep up. They treat every problem like something they can fix personally — right now, today — without realizing that at this scale, personal fixes create new problems faster than they solve old ones.

The freight train demands a different kind of leadership. Not less decisive — but more deliberate.

How Do You Know You're in Transition?

Most owners don't recognize the shift until they're already deep in it. Here are the signals worth watching for:

Quick decisions start feeling harder. Problems that used to have obvious solutions now come with competing priorities attached to them.

Small operational issues cascade faster. One person calling out used to be an inconvenience. Now it affects three other roles and ripples through the whole day.

You start feeling the weight of keeping everything running smoothly while simultaneously trying to grow. The business is demanding more of you at the exact moment you need to be working on it instead of in it.

You find yourself saying "that's not how we do it" more often — which means you have standards but no systems to enforce them consistently.

You're solving the same problems over and over again because nothing is documented and everything lives in someone's head.

If any of those sound familiar, the freight train is already picking up speed. The question is whether you're building the infrastructure to match it.

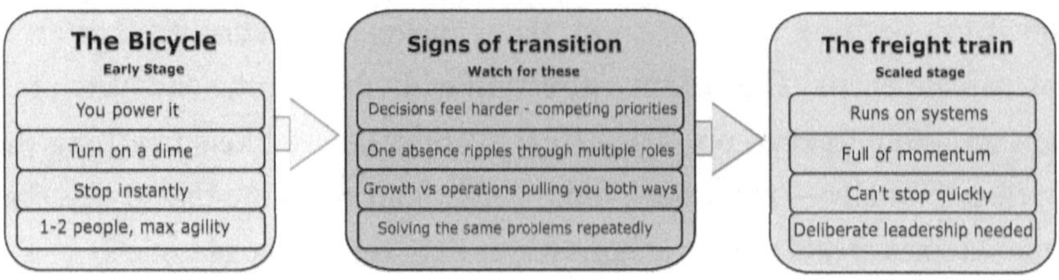

The freight train demands a different kind of leadership - not less decisive, but more deliberate

The COVID Wake-Up Call

Nothing tested the freight train reality harder for me than COVID.

In the first three weeks I lost 40% of my business almost overnight. The world stopped. Several employees quit. The uncertainty was real and it was heavy.

Then, just a month later, demand exploded. People weren't going out. They wanted service delivered to their door. The phone was ringing and orders were coming in — but I had half the team I needed to handle it.

I couldn't hire. People were being paid by the government to stay home or were afraid to work in public. I was caught between surging demand and a shrinking team, with a freight train that had no intention of stopping.

So I did the only thing I could do. I got in the trenches.

I jumped in on the front lines and worked day and night alongside my team. Not because I had a perfect plan. Because the business needed it and my team needed to see it.

When the leader shows up with their sleeves rolled up during the hardest moment the business has ever faced, it sends a message that no speech ever could — *I'm not asking you to do anything I'm not willing to do myself.*

My team responded. We held it together.

The Decision That Changed the Business

With limited capacity and demand outpacing what we could handle, I made a call that felt risky in the moment but turned out to be one of the best decisions I ever made.

I raised our minimum service order by 50%.

The instinct for most owners in that situation is to try to serve everyone — keep every customer, absorb every order, grind through it. I understand that instinct. Turning away business feels like failure, especially when you fought so hard to build it.

But here's what a crisis teaches you that normal operations never quite do: not all customers are equal.

Small orders may require just as much effort to acquire, schedule, and service as large ones — but with a fraction of the revenue. The administrative overhead, the customer touchpoints, the scheduling coordination — it all costs roughly the same regardless of order size. When every hour of labor mattered and capacity was hard to come by, the math on small orders simply didn't work anymore.

Raising the minimum filtered out the lowest-value accounts and protected the capacity to serve the customers worth keeping. We lost some customers. The ones we lost were costing us more than we realized. The ones we kept were exactly who we wanted to be serving.

We came out of that period with fewer customers, higher revenue per order, and a lower cost to serve. The crisis didn't just test the business — it improved it.

I Never Lowered It

Some owners make a bold call during a crisis and quietly walk it back once the pressure eases. I didn't.

The minimum stayed exactly where I set it — and it still is today.

That decision permanently changed the profile of my customer base. Higher average order values. Lower cost to serve. Customers who valued the service enough to meet the standard. What started as a survival move became a strategic foundation I built the rest of the business on.

If you find yourself making a bold call during a difficult moment — and it works — don't walk it back when things get easier. The crisis revealed something true about your business. Honor it.

Revenue Quality Over Revenue Quantity

This lesson extends far beyond a pandemic. It applies any time your business is drinking from the firehose.

When demand exceeds capacity — whether from rapid growth, a staffing shortage, a supply disruption, or an unexpected surge — don't just work harder. Get selective. Protect your best relationships first. Raise your standards if you need to.

The customer who places a small order once a month is not worth the same as the customer who places a large order every week. Treating them identically when resources are constrained is a choice that costs you more than you think.

Constraints are uncomfortable. But they also force clarity. When you can't serve everyone, you learn very quickly who your business actually exists to serve.

Leading Through Uncertainty

One thing the freight train teaches you that nothing else does — your team is watching how you show up when things get hard.

During COVID I didn't have all the answers. Nobody did. But I made sure my team knew where we stood, what we were doing, and that I was right there with them — not in an office somewhere sending updates, but on the floor and in the field doing the work alongside them.

Clear and consistent communication during chaos isn't just good management — it's what keeps people from walking out the door when the pressure is highest.

Here's what I've learned about leading through uncertainty:

Say what you know. Say what you don't know. Tell people what you're doing about it. Then show up and do it.

That's it. It doesn't require a perfect plan. It requires honesty and presence. Your team can handle hard news far better than they can handle silence and uncertainty. In my experience, the owners who held their teams together during COVID weren't the ones with the best answers — they were the ones who showed up.

Build and Fix While the Train Moves

For growing service businesses, there comes a point where the pace of operations accelerates faster than the owner can realistically manage by themselves. The freight train never stops for you to catch up. The systems, processes, and guardrails have to be built while the business is already moving.

That's uncomfortable. It requires discipline to step back and document a process when you're already behind. It requires humility to admit that what worked at ten customers won't work at a hundred. And it requires courage to make bold operational changes when the easier path is to just keep grinding.

But the owners who build the infrastructure while the train is moving are the ones who stay on the tracks when the next crisis hits. And there will always be a next crisis.

Start now. Document one process this week. Create one checklist. Build one guardrail. You don't have to stop the train to fix it — but you do have to start.

We'll talk about how to prepare for the next crisis before it arrives in Principle 8.

Action Checklist:

- Recognize the signs that your business is transitioning from bicycle to freight train
- Stop trying to manage a freight train like a bicycle — the rules have changed
- Document key processes and create simple standard operating procedures
- Build checklists for repeatable tasks so nothing relies solely on memory or one person
- Introduce guardrails and quality standards that protect consistency as volume increases
- Maintain clear, honest, regular communication with your team — especially during rapid change
- Show up visibly during hard moments — leadership by presence is more powerful than leadership by memo
- Audit your customer base — not all revenue is good revenue

- Be willing to make bold operational adjustments when capacity is strained
- If a crisis-driven decision improves your business — keep it
- Prioritize revenue quality over revenue quantity when resources are constrained
- Build systems now, before the next disruption hits

PRINCIPLE 4: Build Systems That Reduce Owner Dependency

There is a version of owning a business that feels like freedom. And there is a version that feels like a prison sentence you gave yourself.

The difference between the two is systems.

A business that runs on the owner's heroics — on their personal involvement in every decision, every process, and every problem — is not a business. It's a job with overhead. It can't scale, it can't be delegated, and it can't be sold for what it's worth. The moment the owner steps away, everything wobbles.

A business built on systems is different. It runs because the processes are documented, the roles are clear, and the people know what to do without being told. The owner can step back — for a day, a week, or permanently — and the operation keeps moving.

That's the goal. And it's more achievable than most owners think.

I Learned This in the Army

Long before I owned a business — before I ever managed a team at a corporation — I learned the value of standard operating procedures serving in the U.S. Army National Guard.

The Army doesn't use SOPs because some consultant recommended them. They use them because in high-pressure situations, when things are moving fast and the stakes are real, people need to be able to execute without stopping to think. The procedure is already in their hands. It's not bureaucracy. It's how you keep people safe and missions on track.

We used to joke that the Army had an SOP for everything — including how to use a toilet. I'm only half kidding. But here's the thing — that culture of documentation and consistency is exactly what makes a large, complex organization function under pressure. And it's exactly what most small businesses are missing.

I carried that discipline into my corporate career, where consistency across large teams wasn't optional — it was the job. And I carried it into my own business, where one person calling out on a busy day could derail the entire operation if the right systems weren't in place.

The Army taught me the value of SOPs early. Thirty years of building and leading teams reinforced the lesson. And my own business proved it repeatedly: under pressure, consistency matters, and clear processes help create it.

If you think SOPs are something only big companies need — think again. They're a survival tool. And the earlier you build them, the easier everything else becomes.

The Patchwork Phase

Most service business owners start the same way. You find a tool that solves one problem. Then another tool for another problem. Then a spreadsheet for something else. Before long you're running five different systems that don't talk to each other, and you're the only person who knows how all the pieces connect.

It works. Until it doesn't.

In my early days I was patching together multiple tools just to manage basic workflow. One for customer reminders. One for invoicing. One for scheduling. It created friction everywhere — for me, for my team, and for my customers. Nothing was seamless. Everything required manual handoffs. And delegation was nearly impossible because no single person could see the whole picture.

The patchwork phase is a natural part of starting out. But recognizing when it's holding you back is critical. If your operation runs on duct tape and tribal knowledge, it will break at the worst possible moment — when you're growing fastest and have the least time to fix it.

The All-In-One Breakthrough

The single biggest operational shift in my business came when I found a software solution that managed the entire workflow in one place — customer management, scheduling, dispatching, invoicing, and communications all integrated and talking to each other.

The difference was immediate and significant.

The customer experience became smoother with less friction at every touch-point. Employees could organize their work and operate more efficiently without constantly switching between tools or waiting for information to be passed along manually. We were able to serve more customers with less effort — not because we worked harder, but because the system removed the obstacles that were slowing everything down.

That's what the right technology does. It doesn't replace good people or good processes. It amplifies them. It removes friction so your team can focus on the work that actually matters — delivering a great experience to every customer, every time.

When you're evaluating tools for your business, stop asking "does this solve my immediate problem?" and start asking "does this fit into a system that my team can run without me?" That's the right filter.

Build the Trust Bridge

Even with the right software in place, delegation still requires trust. And trust is hard for owners who built something from nothing with their own hands.

I know this firsthand. One of the last things I delegated was invoicing and billing — because I wanted to make sure money was being collected and nothing was slipping through the cracks. Billing felt too important, too consequential, too easy to get wrong.

So instead of holding on to it forever, I built what I now think of as a trust bridge.

I created a simple spreadsheet that allowed me to match orders with deposits — a quick daily check that told me whether every order had been paid for without requiring me to do the billing myself. It took minutes to review. It gave me the visibility I needed. And it allowed me to hand the billing process to someone else with confidence.

That's the principle behind every successful delegation: you don't have to choose between letting go completely and doing it yourself. You can build a simple verification system that gives you oversight without requiring your daily involvement. A checklist. A report. A weekly number you review. Something that tells you quickly whether the process is working — without pulling you back into doing the work.

Find your trust bridge for every function you're holding onto. Then cross it.

The Owner Independence Test

Here is a simple and honest test for where your business stands right now.

If you left for two weeks with no phone and no email — what would happen?

Would the business run smoothly? Would your team know what to do? Would customers still be served at the same standard?

Or would everything quietly start to unravel?

Most owners who ask themselves this question honestly don't like the answer. And that's okay — awareness is the first step. But if the business can't function without your daily presence, it's not a people problem. It's a systems problem.

The goal isn't to make yourself unnecessary. It's to make your involvement optional. There's a big difference. An owner who chooses to be involved is powerful. An owner who has to be involved is trapped.

Work toward optional.

SOPs — Simpler Than You Think

A standard operating procedure doesn't have to be a formal document with headers and version numbers. For a small business it can be a one-page checklist, a simple step-by-step guide, or even a short video walkthrough recorded on your phone.

The question it needs to answer is simple: if someone new joined my team tomorrow, could they use this to do the job correctly without asking me?

If the answer is yes — you have an SOP. If the answer is no — you have a gap.

Start with your most critical processes. The ones that happen every day.

The ones where a mistake costs you a customer or creates a safety issue. Document those first. Then work outward from there.

Here's the discipline I'd encourage: every time you find yourself explaining the same thing twice, write it down. Every time you fix the same problem twice, build a process to prevent it. Every repeated conversation is a signal that a system is missing.

A Note on AI Tools

The landscape for small business owners has changed dramatically in just the last few years. AI tools that were once out of reach — in cost, complexity, or both — are now accessible to any owner willing to spend a little time learning them.

I use AI in my own business regularly. Organizing and analyzing data. Creating social media content and images. Building simple tools like schedule trackers. Tasks that used to require hiring someone or outsourcing to an agency can now be handled quickly and inexpensively with the right AI tools.

I'm not suggesting you automate everything or chase every new technology. But if you're still doing manually what a simple AI tool could handle in minutes — you're spending time you don't have on work that doesn't require you.

Start small. Pick one repetitive task that drains your time and find an AI tool that handles it. The time you recover is time you can put back into building the business.

Every tool, every system, every process you build has a compounding effect — not just on your daily operations, but on the ultimate value of what you're building.

The Sellability Connection

Everything in this principle connects directly to the day you decide to sell. In most small business acquisitions, buyers are purchasing systems they can operate without heavy owner dependency. Clean processes, integrated technology, and a team that knows what to do without being told are the foundation of a transferable, valuable business. Build the systems now. Your future self will thank you.

Action Checklist:

- Audit your current tools — are you in the patchwork phase? Is it holding you back?
- Evaluate all-in-one software solutions that integrate your core workflow
- Identify every function you're holding onto and ask why
- Build a trust bridge for each one — a simple verification system that gives you visibility without requiring your involvement
- Document your most critical daily processes first — keep SOPs simple and usable
- Apply the two-week test — if you disappeared, what would break?
- Create a one-page job description for every role with clear responsibilities and standards
- Every time you explain the same thing twice — write it down
- Every time you fix the same problem twice — build a process to prevent it
- Explore AI tools for repetitive tasks that drain your time
- Build your org structure even if it's small — clarity of roles reduces owner dependency
- Measure your progress by how optional your daily involvement becomes — work toward optional, not unnecessary

PRINCIPLE 5: Use Metrics & KPIs for Weekly Accountability

Running a business without tracking metrics is like skipping your annual physical and hoping for the best. And making decisions without understanding your numbers is like a doctor writing a prescription before running a single test.

You might get lucky. Or you might make things significantly worse.

Metrics are the vital signs of your business. They tell you whether the operation is healthy before you feel the symptoms. They catch problems early — while you still have options. And they give you the information you need to make good decisions instead of expensive guesses.

From what I have seen, the owners who build something sustainable aren't necessarily the smartest or the most talented. They're the ones who know their numbers — and actually use them.

A Quick Clarification — Metrics vs. KPIs

You'll hear both terms used interchangeably. Here's a simple way to think about them.

A metric is any number you track. Revenue, error rate, new customers — these are all metrics.

A KPI — Key Performance Indicator — is a metric that is directly tied to a goal that matters. Not every metric is a KPI. But every KPI should be a metric you're watching closely.

For the purposes of this principle, think of your KPIs as the handful of metrics that live on your dashboard — the vital signs you check every single week because they tell you whether the business is on track.

Not All Metrics Are Created Equal

Here's where most business owners go wrong. They either track nothing and fly completely blind, or they track everything and drown in data that never leads to a decision.

The goal isn't to measure everything. The goal is to identify the small set of numbers that together tell you whether your business is healthy. Everything else is noise.

Think of it like a cockpit dashboard. A pilot doesn't monitor every instrument on the panel with equal attention. They know which gauges matter most at any given moment and they scan them regularly. When something moves outside the normal range they investigate. When everything is steady they fly.

Your business needs the same kind of dashboard.

Leading vs. Lagging Indicators

This is one of the most important distinctions in business metrics — and most owners never learn it.

A lagging indicator tells you what has already happened. Revenue, profit, total orders completed — these numbers confirm results. They're valuable but they're backward looking. By the time a lagging indicator looks wrong, the problem has already been developing for weeks.

A leading indicator tells you what's likely to happen. New customers, customer satisfaction scores, inquiry volume — these numbers move before the results do. They give you advance warning while you still have time to respond.

The most powerful dashboards track both. But if you have to choose where to focus your attention — watch your leading indicators. They're the early warning system that lagging indicators can never be.

What I Learned in Corporate

Before I ever owned a business I spent years at a large telecommunications company where metrics were deeply embedded in the culture. I was instrumental in developing sales metrics that drove performance and accountability across large teams.

But the most valuable lesson came from a harder problem — measuring customer retention.

Tracking customers who left was straightforward. The number was right there. But the customers my team was saving — the ones who called to cancel and were talked out of it — were completely invisible. That work was happening every day and nobody could see it. And work that can't be seen can't be measured, rewarded, or improved.

So I built a solution. I created a simple call logging application I called the Saver that allowed representatives to log every save attempt and its outcome. For the first time we could see the full picture — not just who we were losing, but who we were keeping and why.

That tool changed everything. We could identify which representatives were most effective at retention, understand what was working, and coach the rest of the team accordingly.

The explicit lesson I carried into every business I've run since:

Before you can improve something you have to make it visible. Before you can make it visible you have to define what you're measuring and build a way to capture it.

The absence of a metric doesn't mean the activity isn't happening. It means it's invisible. And work that stays invisible becomes much harder to manage consistently.

The things that matter most operationally usually deserve some form of measurement.

Building Your Dashboard

Every small business is different. The specific metrics that matter to you will depend on your industry, your model, and your stage of growth. But here is a framework that applies broadly to any service operation:

Volume — How many units, orders, jobs, or customers did you serve this week? This is your baseline. Everything else is measured against it.

Revenue — What did that volume generate? Track revenue tied directly to output so you can see immediately whether pricing and volume are working together.

Efficiency — How productively is your team working? Output per hour, jobs per shift, tasks completed per day — whatever the relevant unit is in your business. Efficiency metrics tell you whether your operation is getting better or quietly getting worse.

Quality and Accuracy — What is your error rate? How often does something go wrong that shouldn't? Quality metrics keep you honest about the standard you're actually delivering versus the standard you think you're delivering.

Reliability — Are you doing what you promised, when you promised it? Late deliveries, missed appointments, broken commitments — track them as a rate against total activity. A reliability metric is one of the most important signals of customer experience you have.

Customer Satisfaction — Are your customers happy? Surveys, reviews, direct feedback — track sentiment consistently over time. This is a leading indicator that often moves before anything else does. A drop in satisfaction scores is a warning that something needs attention before it shows up in cancellations.

New Customers — Is your business growing? Track new customers weekly, not monthly. Weekly tracking lets you spot trends and respond in real time. This is one of your most important leading indicators.

Customer Losses — Who left and why? Every business loses customers. The question is whether you understand why. A customer who moves away is very different from a customer who left because of a bad experience. Know the difference.

What a Dashboard Actually Looks Like

A dashboard doesn't require expensive software or a technical background. Mine started as a simple spreadsheet — eight rows, one for each vital sign, and a column for every week of the year. Every Monday morning I'd spend fifteen minutes filling in the numbers from the previous week.

That's it. Eight numbers. Fifteen minutes. Every week without exception.

Over time those numbers told me stories I couldn't see any other way. Trends emerged. Patterns became clear. Anomalies stood out immediately because I knew what normal looked like.

Start there. A spreadsheet you actually use every week is worth more than sophisticated software you open once a month.

Sample weekly vital signs dashboard

Volume	Revenue	Efficiency	Error rate
247	$24,180	14.2	1.2%
↑ 8% vs last week	↑ 6% vs last week	units / hour	↑ below 2% target

Reliability	Satisfaction	New signups	Losses
98.4%	4.8 / 5	11	3
		↑ target is 10/wk	investigate reasons

● Anomaly flagged – investigate this week

Customer losses (3) are up from last week's average of 1. Review reasons before assuming seasonal. Net growth this week: +8

Eight vital signs. Fifteen minutes. Every Monday — same time, without exception.

Starting from Zero

If you're just starting out and have no historical data, don't let that stop you. You build a baseline by tracking.

Week one you have one data point. Week four you have something to compare. Week twelve you have a trend. Week fifty-two you have a full year of vital signs that will tell you things about your business you could never learn any other way.

The best time to start tracking was the day you opened. The second best time is today.

The Leaking Bucket

New customer additions minus customer losses give you your net growth number — and it's one of the most revealing metrics in your entire dashboard.

A business adding ten new customers a week but losing eight is not a growing business. It's a leaking bucket. You can pour as much marketing spend as you want into the top and still end up going backwards if you're not watching what's draining out the bottom.

Track both numbers. Watch the gap between them. That gap tells you the real story of where your business is headed.

Using Metrics as a Lever

Here's where metrics stop being just informational and start being operational.

I set a target of twenty new customers per month. By the middle of every month I know whether I'm on track. If customer signups (or new clients, jobs, or accounts — whatever the relevant unit is in your business) are soft and the number is telling me I'm going to fall short, I increase my advertising spend to drive more volume. That assumes the softness is a volume problem. If the numbers suggest something else is going on, I investigate the cause before pulling any lever. If signups are ahead of target and I need to manage capacity, I pull back.

This isn't guesswork. It is a lever connected directly to a metric. I'm not reacting to a problem after it's fully formed — I'm adjusting in real time based on what the numbers are telling me while I still have room to respond.

This is what metrics actually do for you when you use them properly. They don't just tell you what happened. They give you time to change what's about to happen.

Think of it as keeping the freight train on the tracks. You're not waiting to derail. You're watching the gauges and making small adjustments continuously so the big adjustments are never necessary.

Set Your Own Benchmarks

One question every new owner asks is — what does good look like?

The honest answer is that it depends on your business, your market, and your model. Industry benchmarks exist but they vary widely and may not apply to your specific situation.

My advice is to set your own internal benchmarks based on your best performance. When your quality rate hits its highest point — make that the new standard. When your efficiency peaks — chase that number every week. When customer satisfaction scores hit a high — protect that level like it's the floor, not the ceiling.

You are competing against your own best. That's the standard worth chasing.

When the Numbers Tell You Something Is Wrong

One of the most valuable things a metric can do is catch an anomaly — something outside the normal pattern that demands investigation.

My new customer signup rate dropped unexpectedly one month. Not a gradual softening — a noticeable dip that didn't match any seasonal pattern I'd seen before. The number flagged it immediately.

I investigated. It turned out a local social media influencer with a large following had been spreading false information about my business in a community group. The damage was real and it was moving fast.

Because I was watching the metric I caught it early. I took swift legal action, the false claims stopped, and I focused on damage control — leaning on the reputation I had already built with my existing customers and in the community. We recovered.

Without that metric I might have assumed the slowdown was random or seasonal. I might have waited weeks before realizing something was wrong. By then the damage would have been far worse.

The number told me something was wrong before I could feel it. That's exactly what vital signs are supposed to do.

Sharing Metrics with Your Team

Metrics are most powerful when they're not just yours. When the whole team knows the score.

People perform better when they understand what they're working toward and can see whether they're hitting the mark. A team that sees quality scores posted weekly develops a culture of accountability that no amount of supervision can create. A team member who watches their own efficiency improve has something to take pride in.

But how you share metrics matters as much as whether you share them.

Frame metrics as a coaching tool, not a surveillance tool. The goal is improvement, not judgment. When a number is off, the first conversation should be curious — what's happening here, and how do we fix it — not punitive.

There's also an important distinction between team metrics and individual metrics. Posting team quality scores builds collective accountability and shared pride. Publicly ranking individuals against each other can create anxiety, unhealthy competition, and gaming of the numbers. Use individual performance data in one-on-one coaching conversations — not on a public leaderboard.

One more practical note: if you're tracking individual performance data — efficiency, error rates, output — be consistent in how you apply those standards across your team. Inconsistency creates legal exposure and destroys trust. Make sure every employee knows from day one what's being measured and how it will be used. This connects directly back to the clear expectations and 90-day structure we covered in Principle 2.

The Weekly Rhythm

Metrics only work if you review them consistently. Not when you remember. Not when something feels off. Every week — same day, same time, without exception.

I'd recommend Monday morning. You're fresh, the previous week is just closed, and you have the full week ahead to respond to anything the numbers are telling you.

Put it in your calendar as a non-negotiable. Fifteen minutes. Eight numbers. Every week.

That simple discipline — maintained consistently over months and years — will tell you more about your business than any consultant, any course, or any book ever could. Including this one.

The Metrics You Can't Buy

The most important metric I ever built wasn't purchased from a software company. It was a simple spreadsheet I designed myself to verify that every job had been accounted for and paid — a quick daily check that gave me the visibility I needed without requiring my personal involvement in the process.

Some of your most valuable vital signs will be custom — built specifically for your operation because no off-the-shelf tool measures exactly what you need to see. Don't wait for perfect software. A simple spreadsheet that tells you what you need to know is worth more than sophisticated software you never fully use.

One final note on tools. The landscape for small business owners has changed dramatically. AI tools are now accessible to any owner regardless of budget or technical background. I use AI regularly in my own business to help organize and analyze data, spot patterns, and make sense of numbers faster than I ever could manually. If you're staring at a spreadsheet full of weekly numbers and not sure what they're telling you — ask an AI app. You might be surprised how useful a two-minute conversation can be. The goal is insight. Use whatever tool gets you there fastest.

Know your numbers. Watch them consistently. Use them to steer. And when something moves unexpectedly — pay attention. That's where metrics stop being passive reporting and start becoming a leadership tool.

Action Checklist:

- Define the difference between your metrics and your KPIs — focus your dashboard on the vital signs that matter most
- Identify leading indicators in your business — the numbers that warn you before results change
- Build a simple dashboard — eight to ten vital signs reviewed every week
- If you're starting from zero — start tracking today and let the baseline build itself
- Set a weekly rhythm — same day, same time, non-negotiable
- Track new customers and customer losses separately — watch the gap between them
- Set weekly targets for your most critical metrics and review mid-period so you can adjust
- Connect metrics to levers — know in advance what action you'll take when a number moves
- Set internal benchmarks based on your best performance — then chase them
- Investigate every anomaly — good and bad — before assuming you know the cause
- Share team metrics openly — frame them as coaching tools not surveil-

lance

- Use individual performance data in private coaching conversations not public rankings
- Be consistent in how you apply performance standards across your team
- Build custom metrics for anything important that off-the-shelf software doesn't measure
- Explore AI tools to help analyze and interpret your data — the goal is insight, not complexity
- Never confuse the absence of a metric with the absence of activity — if it matters, measure it

PRINCIPLE 6: Keep the Books Clean and Transparent

There is a version of your financial records that tells the truth about what you built. And there is a version that tells a smaller, murkier story — one that saves you a few dollars today and costs you a fortune when it matters most.

Every choice you make about how you manage your books is a vote for one version or the other.

This principle isn't about accounting. It's about protecting and maximizing the value of everything you're working so hard to build.

The Advice Everyone Gets

When I owned my first service business — a laundromat — I got the same advice from more than one fellow business owner.

Pay cash. Keep it off the books. Everyone does it.

And they were right that everyone did it. Cash transactions. Unreported income. A P&L that told a convenient story rather than an accurate one. In an industry where cash businesses were the norm, it was easy to rationalize. The tax savings felt real. The risk felt distant.

I didn't do it.

It was harder. It cost more in the short term. I paid taxes that my competitors were quietly avoiding. There were moments where I wondered whether I was being naive.

Then I sold the business.

The owners who took the cash advice couldn't prove what their businesses were worth. Their books told a story that was smaller than reality — because they had spent years making it smaller on purpose. When it came time to sell, the price reflected the story in the books, not the truth of what they had built. They optimized for avoiding taxes today and paid for it at the exit. The money they saved over the years — they gave it all back at the closing table and then some.

My books told the full, accurate story. The buyer could see it clearly. The price reflected what I had actually built.

Clean books didn't cost me money. They made me money.

The short-term savings of sloppy books will cost you more at the exit than you ever saved along the way.

The Million Dollar Turning Point

Years later, building a second business, I hit a milestone that changed how I thought about everything.

When annual revenue crossed the million dollar mark, something shifted. I could see clearly what I had on my hands — something genuinely valuable. And that clarity changed my behavior.

I got more intentional about the books than I had ever been before. I paid closer attention to personal expenses running through the business and minimized them deliberately. I identified and eliminated anything that could create unnecessary risk — the kind of thing that invites scrutiny, triggers audits, or raises flags with a lender or a buyer.

Not because I had been doing anything wrong. But because I could now see the end game clearly enough to protect it.

The lesson: you don't have to wait until you're planning to sell to start managing your books like someone who is. The earlier you build that discipline, the more valuable the business becomes — and the less painful the process is when the time comes.

What a P&L Actually Is — And Why It Matters

If you're new to business finances, here's a plain-English explanation of the document you'll hear about more than any other.

A Profit and Loss statement (also called a P&L or an income statement) is a summary of your business's revenue and expenses over a specific period of time. It shows what came in, what went out, and what was left over.

At its simplest:

Revenue minus expenses equals net profit or loss.

That's it. But the details inside that simple equation tell an enormously complex story about the health, efficiency, and trajectory of your business. Which expense categories are growing faster than revenue? Which months are strongest? Where is money going that shouldn't be?

A P&L you review regularly (not just at tax time) becomes one of your most powerful management tools. It connects directly to the metrics dashboard we discussed in Principle 5. Your metrics tell you what's happening in real time. Your P&L tells you the financial story of what happened over time. Both are essential. And both only work if the underlying data is clean and accurate.

Get comfortable reading your P&L. It's telling you something every single month.

Setting Up for Success from Day One

Clean books don't happen by accident. They require a deliberate setup — and the earlier you do it, the easier everything becomes.

Here's the practical mechanics of getting it right from the start:

Open a dedicated business checking account. Every business transaction flows through this account. Every payment you receive goes in. Every business expense comes out. Nothing personal touches it.

Get a dedicated business credit card. Use it exclusively for business expenses. Pay it from the business account. Never use it for personal purchases.

Never mix personal and business finances. This is the single most important rule in this entire principle. The moment you start mixing the two — even occasionally, even for convenience — you create a mess that compounds every single month and becomes genuinely painful to untangle.

Pay yourself a defined salary or draw. Decide what you're paying yourself and do it consistently through a documented transaction. If you need to take additional money out of the business, document it as a distribution. Random transfers from the business account to cover personal expenses are the enemy of clean books.

Choose bookkeeping software and use it consistently. There are several accessible, affordable cloud-based options designed specifically for small business owners without accounting backgrounds. The best one is the one you'll actually use every day. Set it up properly from the start — with the right expense categories for your business — and reconcile your accounts every single month without exception.

Understand the difference between a bookkeeper and an accountant — and consider hiring both. A bookkeeper maintains your day-to-day records — categorizing transactions, reconciling accounts, and keeping everything current. An accountant prepares your taxes, provides financial advice, and helps you understand the bigger picture. You often need both. The bookkeeper is the one who keeps things clean on an ongoing basis. Professional bookkeeping for a small business is more affordable than most owners expect — and far cheaper than cleaning up years of messy records when you need them most.

Cash Basis vs. Accrual Accounting

This is a concept worth understanding early — even if you never need to think about it deeply again.

Most small businesses run on cash basis accounting. This means you record income when you actually receive the money and expenses when you actually pay them. It's simple, intuitive, and works well for businesses where money moves in and out relatively quickly.

Accrual accounting records income when it's earned and expenses when they're incurred — regardless of when the cash actually moves. Larger businesses typically use accrual accounting because it gives a more accurate picture of financial performance over time.

For most small business owners, cash basis is the right starting point. But understanding the distinction matters because it affects how you interpret your P&L — and how a buyer or lender might interpret it too. When in doubt, ask your accountant which method is right for your business and your stage of growth.

What Clean Books Actually Mean

Clean books aren't just about accuracy. They're about clarity and defensibility.

A clean set of books tells anyone who looks at them — a lender, a buyer, a partner, an investor, or an auditor — a clear and consistent story about the health and trajectory of your business. Every number is explainable. Every category makes sense. Every transaction has a paper trail.

That clarity builds trust. And in business, trust is worth money.

Here's what clean books actually require in practice:

Be deliberate about what runs through the business. Most small business owners run some personal expenses through the business — it's common practice. But there's a difference between doing it deliberately and documenting it clearly versus doing it carelessly and hoping nobody looks closely. If a personal expense runs through the business, categorize it correctly, keep the receipt, and be prepared to explain it. A buyer's accountant will find it. The question is whether you're ready with a clean explanation or scrambling to remember what it was.

Handle cash transactions with the same discipline as everything else. Cash is not invisible. Gaps in your revenue picture are noticeable — to buyers, to lenders, and to auditors. Untracked cash doesn't just create tax risk. It creates a story problem. If your deposits don't tell a coherent story about your revenue, you'll spend enormous energy during any due diligence process trying to explain the gaps. It's not worth it.

Categorize expenses accurately and consistently. Misclassified expenses distort your P&L in ways that are hard to explain later. Inconsistent categorization makes your books harder to defend and easier to attack. Pick a category structure that reflects your business and stick to it.

Keep receipts and documentation for everything. The documentation is the proof. A number without documentation is just a claim. A number with documentation is a fact. In any transaction involving your business — a sale, a loan, a partnership — facts are worth more than claims.

Clean Books Are a Valuation Multiplier

Here's something most owners don't realize until they're sitting across from a buyer or a banker:

Clean books don't just protect you. They increase what your business is worth.

A business with three years of clean, consistent, well-documented financials commands a higher valuation multiple than an identical business with messy books. The numbers might be the same — but the confidence they create is not. A buyer who trusts your books negotiates less aggressively. A lender who trusts your books approves faster. A partner who trusts your books commits more readily.

Every dollar you spend keeping your books clean and every hour you spend maintaining that discipline is an investment in the confidence of everyone who will ever need to evaluate what you built.

That confidence has a dollar value. It shows up at the closing table.

Owner Add-Backs and Normalization

This is a concept that most small business owners don't encounter until they're trying to sell — and by then it's too late to go back and fix it.

When a buyer evaluates a small business, they don't just look at the bottom line profit. They look at what's called the Seller's Discretionary Earnings — the true economic benefit to the owner, adjusted for expenses that were personal in nature or non-recurring.

Common add-backs include the owner's salary, personal expenses run through the business, one-time costs that won't repeat, and non-cash expenses like depreciation.

Here's why this matters for how you keep your books:

The cleaner and more clearly documented your add-backs are, the more defensible your normalized earnings number is. A buyer's advisor will scrutinize every add-back. If you can produce documentation for each one — receipts, categorization, a clear explanation of why it belongs in the add-back — the negotiation is straightforward. If you can't, every add-back becomes a point of contention that chips away at the price.

When I prepared my first business for sale, I learned this firsthand. The owners who struggled most in that process weren't the ones with the weakest businesses. They were the ones with the messiest books. They couldn't tell a clean story about what they had built because the records didn't support one.

Document everything. Categorize everything correctly. And when you run a personal expense through the business — note it, track it, and be ready to explain it clearly.

A Note on Payroll and Employee Classification

Clean books include clean payroll records — and this is an area where small business owners make expensive mistakes more often than any other.

Document hours accurately. Maintain consistent pay records. Ensure your withholding is correct. And pay close attention to how you classify the people who work for you.

The distinction between an employee and an independent contractor matters enormously — legally, financially, and at sale time. Employees receive a W-2. Contractors receive a 1099. The difference affects taxes, benefits, liability, and your obligations as an employer.

Misclassifying employees as contractors is one of the most common audit triggers for small businesses — and one of the most expensive mistakes to correct after the fact. If you're unsure how to classify someone, ask your accountant before you make the decision, not after.

Clean payroll records also matter when you sell. A buyer who acquires a business with employees is inheriting those employment relationships. Messy payroll records, undocumented compensation agreements, or classification problems can complicate or kill a deal just as easily as messy financial records.

The Audit Risk You Don't Need

Beyond the sale, clean books protect you from something most owners don't think about until it happens — unnecessary scrutiny from tax authorities.

Certain patterns in small business financials are known triggers. Inconsistent revenue reporting. Expenses that don't match the nature of the business. Unusually high cash transactions without corresponding deposits. Personal expenses that look like business expenses without documentation.

None of these things mean you did something wrong. But they create the appearance of something worth looking at — and an audit, even one you survive cleanly, costs time, money, and stress that nobody needs.

The best audit protection isn't a clever accountant. It's books that are clean enough that there's nothing interesting to find.

How Long to Keep Your Records

Most owners don't think about document retention until they need a record they no longer have.

As a general guideline — keep tax returns and supporting documentation for at least seven years. Keep payroll records for at least four years. Keep contracts, leases, and major purchase records for the life of the agreement plus several years beyond.

These aren't just legal protections. They're business assets. The ability to produce a clean record from three years ago — during a sale, an audit, or a dispute — is worth more than the storage space it takes up.

When in doubt, keep it. Digital storage is cheap. Missing documentation is expensive.

Build Your Due Diligence Folder Now

Here is one of the most practical things you can do today regardless of whether you ever plan to sell.

Create a folder — digital or physical — where you maintain an organized collection of your most important business documents. Tax returns for the last three years. Monthly P&Ls. Payroll records. Key contracts. Equipment and asset records. Insurance policies. Any agreements with vendors, landlords, or partners.

Call it your due diligence folder. Add to it regularly. Keep it current.

When a buyer, a lender, or a partner asks for documentation — and they will — you hand them the folder instead of spending weeks hunting for records. That alone sends a powerful signal about how you run your business.

The owners who are most prepared for a transaction are rarely the ones who scrambled to get ready. They're the ones who were already ready without knowing exactly when they'd need to be.

The Monthly Financial Ritual

Metrics get a weekly review. Books deserve a monthly one.

Set a recurring date — the first Monday of every month works well — and block thirty minutes to review your financial position. Look at the same things every time:

Revenue versus the prior month and the prior year. Are you growing?

Expense categories versus prior periods. Is anything trending in the wrong direction?

Net profit. What did the business actually keep?

Cash position. What does the bank account look like and what's coming due?

Any anomalies — anything that doesn't look right or that you can't immediately explain.

That thirty minute monthly ritual — maintained consistently over months and years — builds a level of financial fluency that most small business owners never develop. You'll stop being surprised by your own numbers. You'll catch problems early. And you'll be able to talk about your business finances with confidence in any conversation — with a lender, a buyer, or a partner.

Financial fluency is a competitive advantage. Build it deliberately.

Action Checklist:

- Open dedicated business banking and credit accounts — separate everything from day one
- Never mix personal and business finances — not even occasionally
- Pay yourself a defined consistent salary or draw — document everything beyond that
- Choose bookkeeping software and use it every day — reconcile monthly without exception
- Understand the difference between a bookkeeper and an accountant — consider hiring both
- Categorize every expense accurately and consistently
- Keep receipts and documentation for everything
- Handle cash transactions with the same discipline as everything else
- Learn to read your P&L — review it monthly not just at tax time
- Understand cash basis versus accrual accounting and which applies to your business
- Document personal expenses run through the business clearly — be ready to explain every one
- Understand Seller's Discretionary Earnings and start building a clean normalization story now
- Classify employees and contractors correctly — ask your accountant if you're unsure

- Maintain clean payroll records consistently
- Keep financial and legal records for the appropriate retention periods — when in doubt keep it
- Build and maintain a due diligence folder starting today
- Set a monthly financial review ritual — same date, same time, every month
- Remember: clean books are not just protection — they are a valuation multiplier

PRINCIPLE 7: Raise Prices by Delivering Superior Value

Most small business owners think about pricing as a math problem. Calculate your costs. Add a margin. Set a number.

This isn't wrong. But it's incomplete.

The owners who command the best prices — who raise them consistently without losing the customers worth keeping — don't win on math. They win on value. They win on trust. They win on the experience they deliver every single time, and the way that experience makes customers feel.

This principle is about building a business that earns the right to charge more — because the value it delivers is undeniable.

The Early Days — Do Whatever It Takes

When I started my first service business I had no reputation, no referrals, and no budget. What I had was hustle and a willingness to look slightly ridiculous in the pursuit of customers.

I hired a clown on stilts to walk around a local university campus handing out flyers. He was eventually asked to leave. I'm not sure the flyers generated a single customer — but it cost almost nothing and it made people laugh, which felt like something.

I bought a vinyl cutter and a heat press and made branded uniforms for my staff myself. Not because I had a marketing budget for it — but because I understood instinctively that how your team looks affects how customers perceive the service. I used the same equipment to make signs and vehicle lettering. Every van on the road was a rolling billboard for the business —

and I made every decal by hand because I had no money to pay someone else to do it.

A professional appearance signals a professional operation. Even when everything else was held together with duct tape, the uniforms and the lettered vans said — we take this seriously.

That instinct — that brand and presentation matter even when you're just starting out — came before I had any budget to act on it professionally. It came from understanding that customers form impressions before they experience the service. What they see first shapes what they expect. And what they expect shapes how they feel about what they receive.

I tried every grassroots tactic I could think of. Some worked. Most didn't. All of them taught me something.

And then something shifted.

The phone started ringing from people who had heard about us from someone they trusted. Not from a flyer. Not from an ad. From a friend who said — you have to try this, they're incredible.

That was the moment I understood what actually drives a service business.

The Turning Point

No marketing tactic I ever tried came close to matching the power of a genuinely delighted customer telling someone they cared about.

Word of mouth didn't just generate leads. It generated the right leads — people who arrived already trusting us because someone they respected had vouched for us. They were easier to serve, more loyal from the start, and more likely to become promoters themselves.

The math was undeniable. The cheapest customer I ever acquired came from a referral. The most expensive came from paid advertising. And the referral customer stayed longer, complained less, and sent more people our way.

The best marketing I ever did wasn't a campaign. It was delivering an exceptional service every single time and trusting that people would notice.

The Philosophy That Changed Everything

Early in my corporate career a mentor said something that has stayed with me through every business I've owned since.

We are a customer service organization that happens to offer telecommunications services.

I've applied that philosophy to every business I've run. We are a customer service organization that happens to offer a service. The service is the vehicle. The experience is the product.

That reframe changes everything about how you make decisions. It changes how you hire. It changes how you train. It changes how you handle complaints, how you communicate with customers, and what you consider a win.

When a customer calls with a problem, a service organization asks — how do we fix this? When a customer leaves, a service organization asks — what could we have done differently? When a customer goes out of their way to say thank you, a service organization asks — how do we make sure every customer feels that way?

This isn't soft thinking. It's a competitive advantage that most businesses never develop because it requires genuine commitment rather than a policy manual.

Decide what kind of organization you are. Then build everything around that decision.

And make sure your team knows it. The customer service philosophy isn't just yours — it belongs to everyone who represents your business. It goes into your hiring conversations, your onboarding, your 90-day check-ins, and your coaching. The people on your front line are the ones delivering the experience. They need to understand not just what to do — but why it matters.

Satisfaction vs. Delight

There is a meaningful difference between a customer who is satisfied and a customer who is delighted — and it's worth understanding clearly.

Satisfaction means you did what you promised. The service was delivered on time. The quality was acceptable. The customer got what they paid for.

Fine. Forgettable.

Delight means you did something they didn't expect. Something small that made them feel like they mattered — like they were seen as a person, not a transaction. That's memorable. That's what people tell their friends about.

In a service business, satisfaction keeps customers. Delight creates promoters.

The difference between the two is often smaller than you think. It doesn't require grand gestures or expensive programs. It requires attention and intention.

I sent handwritten letters to customers. Holiday cards. Occasional gift baskets. I reached out when they weren't expecting it — not to sell anything, just to say we appreciate you. Something as simple as a note that says *"We just wanted you to know how much we value your business — thank you for trusting us"* costs almost nothing and lands in a way that a promotional email never will.

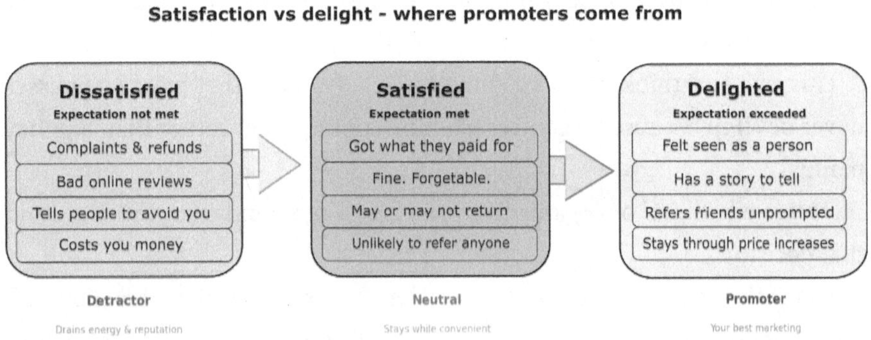

Satisfaction vs delight - where promoters come from

Dissatisfied
Expectation not met
Complaints & refunds
Bad online reviews
Tells people to avoid you
Costs you money
Detractor
Drains energy & reputation

Satisfied
Expectation met
Got what they paid for
Fine. Forgetable.
May or may not return
Unlikely to refer anyone
Neutral
Stays while convenient

Delighted
Expectation exceeded
Felt seen as a person
Has a story to tell
Refers friends unprompted
Stays through price increases
Promoter
Your best marketing

The gap between satisfied and delighted is where promoters — and your best growth — come from. By resolving detractors' problems quickly, thoroughly, and with genuine care, you can turn them into loyal promoters.

Empower Your Team to Delight

The delight philosophy only works if it lives in your culture — not just in your head.

A frontline employee who wants to do something special for a customer but has to ask permission every time will eventually stop trying. Empower your team to make small decisions that create memorable moments — within reasonable parameters. A complimentary add-on. A handwritten thank you.

Going slightly beyond what was asked because the situation called for it.

When a team member creates a genuine delight moment — call attention to it. Tell the story at a team meeting. Recognize it publicly. The behavior you celebrate is the behavior you get more of. If delight is a value, the people who live it deserve to be acknowledged for it.

Look for ways to delight your customers — not just satisfy them. The gap between those two words is where promoters are made.

Sometimes the most powerful delight moments aren't planned at all.

The Goodwill Story

Early in my business a call came in from a group of people who wanted to purchase a gift card for a woman in their community who was going through cancer treatment. She had children. She couldn't work. They wanted to do something meaningful for her.

I doubled the value of the gift card.

Not because it was good marketing. Because it was the right thing to do.

She recovered. She resumed her life. And she became one of the most loyal, vocal promoters my business ever had — someone who told everyone she knew about us not because we asked her to, but because we had shown her who we were at a moment that mattered.

That's the power of a customer service organization. You don't just serve customers. You show up for people. And people remember how you made them feel long after they've forgotten what you charged them.

You can't manufacture moments like that. But you can create the conditions for them by building a business that genuinely cares — and making sure everyone on your team understands that caring is part of the job.

Promoters and Detractors

Not all customers are equal. And understanding the difference is one of the most important skills you can develop as a service business owner.

Promoters are customers who tell people about you. They refer friends, leave reviews, defend you when someone criticizes you, and generate new business without being asked. They are your most valuable asset — more valuable than any marketing budget you'll ever have. Invest in these relationships. Delight them consistently. Make them feel like insiders.

Detractors are the opposite. They drain your energy, generate complaints disproportionate to their value, and sometimes actively work against you. Not because they're bad people — but because the fit was never right, or the expectation was never realistic, or something went wrong that couldn't be fully repaired.

Your goal is simple: build as many promoters as possible. And don't let detractors live inside your head.

One way to measure where you stand is to ask your customers directly. A single question — *"How likely are you to recommend us to a friend or colleague?"* — tracked consistently over time, gives you a pulse on your promoter base that no other metric quite captures. When that number trends up, you're building something. When it trends down, something needs attention.

Building a Referral Culture

Referrals don't always happen automatically — even from your most delighted customers. Sometimes people need a gentle nudge and a simple way to act on their goodwill.

Make it easy. Tell your best customers that referrals are the greatest compliment they can give you. Consider a simple referral program — a credit, a discount, a thank you gift — that acknowledges the gesture and rewards the loyalty. It doesn't need to be elaborate. A handwritten note that says *"Thank you for sending your friend our way — it means everything to us"* is often enough.

The owners who build the strongest referral cultures aren't the ones with the most sophisticated programs. They're the ones whose customers feel so genuinely valued that telling friends feels natural — almost inevitable.

Customer Lifetime Value: Why Delight Is Worth More Than It Costs

Here's a concept that changes how you think about every delight gesture, every complaint resolution, and every price decision.

Customer lifetime value is the total revenue a customer generates over the entire relationship with your business. Not their first transaction. Their tenth. Their fiftieth. Plus every customer they referred who did the same.

A customer who stays five years and refers three friends is worth dramatically more than their first invoice suggests. When you understand that number — even roughly — the math on delight changes completely. A holiday card that costs three dollars. A doubled gift card. An extra hour spent making a complaint right. These aren't costs. They're investments in a relationship that compounds over time.

Before you dismiss a delight gesture as too expensive — calculate what that customer is actually worth to you over a lifetime. Then decide.

Service Recovery: Your Secret Weapon

Here's something counterintuitive that experience taught me: some of my best five-star reviews started with a service problem.

Not despite the problem — because of how we handled it.

A customer whose complaint is resolved quickly, genuinely, and with care becomes more loyal than a customer who never had a problem. They have a story to tell — not just "they were good" but "something went wrong and they made it right immediately and I've never felt more valued as a customer." That story is more powerful than any five-star review from a smooth transaction.

This is called service recovery — and it's one of the most underrated competitive advantages in a service business.

When something goes wrong — and it will — your response in that moment defines your relationship with that customer more than anything else you've ever done for them. Move fast. Take responsibility. Fix it completely. Follow up to make sure.

Don't just aim to resolve the complaint. Aim to create a story worth telling.

Handling Irate Customers: Developing Thick Skin

Early in my career, working as an inbound call center representative, a customer called to complain about a service technician parked across the street with headlights shining into his windows. He was upset. I tried to relate — I mentioned that I lived near a parking lot and understood how annoying lights could be.

His response: *"I don't care whether you live or die."*

I was young. I was trying to help. And I got hit with that.

I stayed calm. I contacted the technician and resolved the situation. And I learned something that has served me in every customer interaction since — sometimes you have to take it.

Not because the customer is right. Not because the behavior is acceptable. But because your job in that moment is to solve the problem, not to win the argument. Professionalism under pressure is a skill. It has to be developed deliberately because it doesn't come naturally to anyone.

If a customer is venting — let them vent. Acknowledge their frustration. Fix what can be fixed. Move on.

That said — thick skin has limits. There is a difference between professional resilience and absorbing genuine abuse. Train your team to de-escalate and stay composed. But also make clear that there are limits — and that you have their back when those limits are crossed. Allowing abusive behavior to continue unchallenged sends a message to your team that their wellbeing matters less than the revenue. It doesn't. Address it.

Responding to Reviews

Bad reviews are not the end of the world. How you respond to them is what matters.

When a negative review comes in — read it carefully before you respond. Is there a legitimate lesson in it? Take the lesson. Acknowledge it. Show the reader — because your response is public — that you take feedback seriously and act on it.

Here's a simple framework that works:

Acknowledge the experience without being defensive. Apologize for the frustration regardless of fault. Offer to make it right and take the conversation offline. Then follow through.

What you never do is argue publicly. Even if you're right. Especially if you're right. A defensive response to a bad review tells every potential customer reading it more about you than the original complaint ever could.

For positive reviews — respond to those too. A brief, genuine thank you that acknowledges something specific in the review shows that real people are behind the business. It reinforces the relationship with the reviewer and signals to everyone else that you pay attention and you care.

When to Fire a Customer

Here's something most business books won't tell you: sometimes the right business decision is to let a customer go.

Not every customer is worth keeping. Before you apply a remedy to a difficult situation, assess it critically.

What is this customer worth to the business? A high-value, long-term customer who has a legitimate complaint deserves a significant remedy — and the investment to make it right. A low-value customer who is chronically difficult, abusive to your team, or impossible to satisfy deserves a different calculation entirely.

What is the risk if they leave unhappy? Some customers will take to social media regardless of what you do. Others will accept a reasonable resolution and move on. Know your customer well enough to assess which situation you're in.

Have you done everything reasonable to make it right? If yes — and the customer is still unreasonable — you've fulfilled your obligation. At that point, continuing to absorb the relationship is a choice, not a requirement.

Sometimes the most professional thing you can do is end the relationship cleanly. A brief, respectful conversation that says this doesn't seem to be the right fit goes a long way. You're not attacking the customer. You're acknowledging reality.

Firing a customer protects your team from abuse. It protects your culture from the corrosive effect of chronic negativity. And it frees up the energy and capacity you were spending on the wrong relationship to invest in the right ones.

The customers worth keeping know they're valued. The customers not worth keeping often know it too.

Earning the Right to Raise Prices

Here's where everything in this principle connects to the word in the title — prices.

Most owners are afraid to raise prices. They worry about losing customers. They worry about the phone call from someone who noticed the increase. They keep prices flat long after the cost of delivering the service has risen — quietly eroding their margins while telling themselves they'll address it next year.

The antidote to that fear is value.

When your customers trust you completely — when they feel genuinely cared for, consistently delighted, and confident that you will show up for them when it matters — raising prices becomes a very different conversation. You're not asking them to pay more for the same thing. You're asking them to continue investing in a relationship that has earned their trust and delivered on its promises.

Customers who feel like promoters don't leave over a price increase. They understand that good things cost more than average things. They've experienced the difference and they've decided you're worth it.

Customers who feel like transactions do leave. And honestly — if a modest price increase is enough to lose them, they were never your best customers anyway.

Businesses that compete on price alone are in a race to the bottom. There will always be someone willing to charge less. Businesses that compete on experience and relationship have pricing power that commodity providers will never have — because the relationship isn't something a competitor can undercut.

During a period of significant operational pressure I raised my minimum service order by 50%. I lost some customers. The ones I lost were the ones with the smallest orders and the highest cost to serve. The ones who stayed were exactly who I wanted to be serving. I never walked it back — and the business was stronger for it.

That's what earning the right to raise prices looks like. You build the value first. Then you charge what it's worth.

How to Communicate a Price Increase

Most owners dread this conversation. It doesn't have to be difficult.

The key is to frame the increase around value delivered — not around your costs or your needs. Your customers don't care that your expenses went up. They care about what they're getting and whether it's worth what they're paying.

A price increase communication that works sounds something like this:

"We've been committed to delivering the highest quality service to you and we want to make sure that commitment never wavers. To continue investing in the

people, equipment, and standards that make that possible, we'll be adjusting our pricing on [date]. We're grateful for your trust and we don't take it for granted."

Short. Honest. Value-focused. No apology for charging what you're worth.

Give adequate notice — thirty days is typically appropriate for a service business. Be consistent — apply the increase across your customer base rather than selectively. And don't over-explain. A brief, confident communication respects your customer's intelligence and signals that you believe in what you're delivering.

As a general guideline — a modest annual increase in the range of three to five percent tied to inflation and rising costs is reasonable and defensible. Larger increases — ten percent or more — require stronger justification and more careful communication. Whatever the amount, the framing matters as much as the number.

Action Checklist:

- Define your business as a customer service organization first — everything else is secondary
- Embed the customer service philosophy into hiring, onboarding, and coaching — not just your own mindset
- Invest in brand and presentation from day one — even on a shoestring budget
- Look for ways to delight customers not just satisfy them — small consistent gestures build promoters
- Send handwritten notes, holiday cards, or unexpected communications — personal touches leave lasting impressions
- Empower your team to make small delight decisions within reasonable parameters
- Recognize and celebrate team members who create delight moments
- Build a referral culture — make it easy for delighted customers to send people your way
- Consider a simple referral program — even a thank you note formalizes the gesture
- Track your promoter base — ask customers how likely they are to refer

you and watch that number over time

- Understand customer lifetime value — calculate what your best customers are actually worth before dismissing any retention investment
- When something goes wrong — use it. Brilliant service recovery creates more loyal customers than smooth transactions
- Develop thick skin — learn to separate the person venting from the problem that needs solving
- Know the limits — support your team when customer behavior crosses the line
- Respond to every review professionally — positive and negative
- Never argue publicly with a negative reviewer — take it offline
- Assess difficult customer situations critically — what is this customer worth and what is the right remedy?
- Don't be afraid to fire a customer who is abusive, chronically unreasonable, or costs more than they contribute
- Build value consistently before raising prices — earn the right first
- Review your pricing annually — a three to five percent increase tied to inflation is reasonable and defensible
- Communicate price increases with confidence — frame around value delivered not your costs
- Give adequate notice and apply increases consistently across your customer base
- Remember: businesses that compete on experience have pricing power that commodity providers never will

PRINCIPLE 8: Always Have a Backup Plan — Business Continuity

You cannot prepare for everything. COVID proved that to every business owner on the planet simultaneously.

But here's what I've learned from years of running service businesses and from a corporate career that required formal business continuity planning at scale — the owners who recover fastest from disruption aren't the ones who predicted exactly what would happen. They're the ones who built resilient operations before anything went wrong.

A plan won't prevent the next crisis. It will determine how quickly you get through it.

What Corporate Taught Me

Early in my corporate career I was part of a large telecommunications organization that took business continuity planning seriously — not as a theoretical exercise but as an operational discipline.

The drills were exhausting at the time. Conference calls every two hours around the clock during a disaster scenario. Detailed plans for every conceivable disruption. Redundant systems. Backup locations. Escalation protocols. At the time it felt like overkill.

Then I watched those plans work in real situations — keeping services running for customers who depended on them when everything around the operation was chaotic. I understood then why the preparation mattered.

A telecommunications company has an obligation to stay operational because people depend on it. So does your service business. Your customers have built their lives around the convenience and reliability you provide. When disruption hits — and it will — your job is to keep the train moving as smoothly as possible.

That corporate discipline shaped how I think about continuity in every business I've run since. Not with the same formality — a small business doesn't need a fifty page disaster recovery document. But with the same intentionality.

Start with Your Key Stakeholders

The first question in any continuity plan is simple: who do I absolutely need besides myself to keep this operation running?

Not everyone on your team. The critical few — the people whose sudden absence would create a genuine operational hole. Identify those roles clearly. Then ask a harder question: what happens if one of them leaves tomorrow?

One person leaving cannot cripple your entire operation. If it can, that's not a people problem. It's a systems and planning problem.

For every critical role you need at minimum:

Documented processes — so the institutional knowledge that lives in that person's head is captured somewhere accessible.

A cross-trained backup — someone else on the team who understands the role well enough to cover it temporarily.

A pipeline — someone you're actively developing who could step into the role with reasonable preparation if needed.

This doesn't mean you're planning to lose people. It means you're building an operation that doesn't depend on any single person, including yourself. Which is exactly what Principle 4 was about. Continuity planning and systems building are the same discipline looked at from two different angles.

Culture Is Your Best Continuity Plan

Here's something I've learned from having key employees leave over the years — and yes, it happened more than once, and yes, it created a hole each time.

The hole was always temporary.

A solid team pulls together during difficult times. They cover for each other. They step up without being asked. They protect what they've helped build. That kind of loyalty isn't luck. It's culture. Culture is something you build deliberately over years of investing in your people, treating them with respect, and creating an environment worth belonging to.

A reputable business doesn't just attract good customers. It attracts good employees too. People want to work somewhere they're proud of. Somewhere with a track record of doing things right. Somewhere that will treat them well when things get hard.

That reputation — built through Principle 2 and Principle 7 and every interaction your team has ever had — becomes a continuity asset when disruption hits. The next good person finds you more easily because of who you are. And the people already on your team fight harder for you because of how you've treated them.

Invest in your culture consistently. It will carry you through moments that no plan could fully anticipate.

Protect Your Critical Systems

Your operation runs on systems — software, equipment, vehicles, facilities, vendor relationships. Every one of those is a potential point of failure. Your continuity plan needs to address each of them.

Software and technology — What happens if your primary software goes down tomorrow? Do you have a backup provider identified? Do you know how long migration would take? A single software vendor holding your entire operation hostage is a vulnerability worth addressing before it becomes a crisis. Know your options. Keep your data backed up and accessible. And read your contracts carefully — cancellation terms, data portability, and service level agreements matter more than most owners realize when they're signing up.

Equipment — What is your most critical piece of equipment and what happens if it fails? Do you have a maintenance relationship that prioritizes your repairs? Do you have a backup source for the same function? For businesses with vehicles on the road — what is your protocol when a vehicle breaks down mid-job? The answers to these questions should be written down before you need them.

Vendors and suppliers — What happens if your primary supplier can't deliver?

Identify backup vendors for your most critical inputs before you're desperate for them. Strong relationships with multiple suppliers give you options. Single-source dependency gives you vulnerability.

Facility Security: Don't Overlook Your Location

This one is easy to miss until it becomes urgent.

Where you operate from is part of your continuity plan. A month to month lease arrangement might feel flexible and low-commitment — but it creates a vulnerability that can become a genuine crisis. The landlord can change terms, sell the property, or decide not to renew with very little notice. Suddenly you're facing a relocation in the middle of running an operation that never stops.

I learned this firsthand. A facility arrangement that worked well operationally but lacked the security of a formal long-term agreement created uncertainty and urgency I hadn't fully anticipated.

Get your facility position as secure as possible. A multi-year lease with clear renewal terms is far better than month to month. Ownership is better still if it's achievable. And if your operation depends on access to someone else's facility or equipment — get that arrangement in writing with enough notice provisions to give you time to respond if it changes.

The freight train needs a track to run on. Make sure yours is secure.

Weather and Predictable Disruptions

Here's a continuity topic that most business books ignore but that every service business in the northeast knows intimately — weather.

Not every disruption is a catastrophe. Some of them are just Tuesday in February.

A significant snowstorm, an ice event, extreme heat, flooding — these are predictable disruptions that hit service businesses regularly and often without much warning. Having a clear protocol for weather events isn't an overreaction. It's operational discipline.

For businesses with vehicles on the road, the decision to pull off is one of the most important calls you'll make. The financial cost of a lost service day is real — but it is finite and recoverable. The cost of a serious accident or an employee injury is neither. Make the call early. Communicate with customers proactively. Have a rescheduling protocol ready to execute.

The same principle applies to any predictable disruption in your market — seasonal slowdowns, local events that affect your territory, recurring demand surges that strain capacity. These aren't surprises. They're patterns. Plan for them before they arrive.

Build a simple weather and disruption protocol into your operations:

When do you make the call to pull vehicles or suspend service?

Who makes that call and how is it communicated to the team?

How do you notify customers and what do you offer them?

How do you reschedule efficiently without creating a backlog that strains the following week?

A documented protocol means the decision gets made the same way every time — calmly, in advance, without the pressure of the moment driving a bad choice.

Insurance — The Coverage Most Owners Miss

Insurance is not a sexy topic. It's also not optional.

A service business with employees, vehicles, and customer relationships has real exposure — and the wrong insurance decision can turn a manageable incident into an existential one. Here's the coverage picture every service business owner needs to understand:

General liability insurance — the foundation. Covers bodily injury and property damage claims arising from your business operations. Non-negotiable from day one.

Commercial auto insurance — if your business uses vehicles, personal auto insurance is not sufficient. Personal policies explicitly exclude business use. A driver in a company vehicle — or a personal vehicle used for business purposes — needs commercial coverage. One serious accident without it is financially devastating.

Workers compensation — mandatory in most states if you have employees. Covers medical expenses and lost wages if an employee is injured on the job. A service business with people working in the field has real exposure here. Don't operate without it.

Business interruption insurance — this is the one most owners never think about until they need it. Covers lost revenue and ongoing operating expenses if your business is forced to shut down temporarily due to a covered event. Given that a service business generates no revenue when it can't operate — this coverage deserves serious consideration.

Umbrella policy — an additional layer of liability coverage beyond your general liability and auto limits. Relatively inexpensive for the protection it provides. When something goes seriously wrong — a major accident, a significant lawsuit — umbrella coverage is what stands between the incident and your personal assets.

Employment practices liability — covers claims from employees related to wrongful termination, discrimination, and harassment. As your team grows this becomes increasingly relevant. One employment claim without this coverage can be enormously expensive.

Review your coverage annually with an insurance professional who understands your businesses. As your revenue, team size, and asset base grow — your coverage needs to grow with them. The policy that was right at year one may leave significant gaps by year five.

Financial Continuity

A business that runs out of cash during a crisis doesn't get a second chance. Financial resilience is as important as operational resilience — and it requires the same kind of advance planning.

Cash reserve — we covered this in Principle 1 but it bears repeating in the context of continuity. Two to three months of operating expenses in a dedicated reserve account that you don't touch unless it's a genuine emergency. This is your first line of financial defense when disruption hits.

Line of credit — secure one while your financials are strong and you don't urgently need it. A line of credit sitting unused is one of the most valuable things a small business owner can have. It's not debt — it's options. When a crisis hits and you need to bridge a gap, the ability to draw on a line of credit quickly — without scrambling to qualify under pressure — can be the difference between surviving and not.

Accounts receivable discipline — slow collections during a crisis compound the problem dramatically. Invoice immediately. Follow up consistently. Don't let receivables pile up during good times because they become a critical lifeline during bad ones. The money customers owe you is your money — collect it promptly.

Diversified revenue — if the majority of your revenue comes from a small number of customers, the loss of one or two accounts is itself a continuity event. Spreading revenue across a broader customer base reduces that concentration risk. No single customer should represent so large a share of your revenue that losing them threatens the operation.

Vendor relationships — strong relationships with your key vendors built on consistent payment and mutual respect buy goodwill that matters when you need flexibility. A vendor who knows you well and trusts you is far more likely to work with you on terms during a difficult period than one who only hears from you when you need something.

The Human Side of Continuity

Every continuity plan I've ever seen focuses on systems, finances, and operations. Very few address the disruption that is hardest to plan for and most devastating when it arrives — the human kind.

Some of the most significant moments of crisis I've ever navigated had nothing to do with equipment failures or software outages or cash flow gaps. They had everything to do with people — scared, grieving, broken-hearted people who still had to show up and do their jobs.

When the World Stopped

On September 11th 2001 I was working in a large call center when the news broke. Within minutes the atmosphere changed completely. Agents were crying at their desks. Others were frozen — staring at screens, unable to speak. Many simply couldn't take calls. The phones kept ringing because the world outside our walls still needed service — but the people inside our walls were not okay.

There was no manual for that moment. No SOP. No business continuity plan that covered what to do when your entire team is watching the world fall apart in real time.

What it required was quick thinking, genuine sensitivity, and the willingness to put people before productivity. We acknowledged what was happening. We gave people space to feel it. We made adjustments to how we operated that day because the alternative — pretending it wasn't happening and demanding normal performance — would have been both inhumane and ineffective.

The lesson I carried from that day: there are moments when leadership means setting the operational agenda aside entirely and simply being present for your people. Those moments are rare. When they arrive you'll know. Don't miss them by being too focused on the business to see the humans in front of you.

When Grief Comes to Work

Later in my corporate career a beloved member of my team died suddenly and unexpectedly. The grief that swept through the department was immediate and profound. These were people who had worked alongside this person every day — who knew their laugh, their habits, their stories. The loss wasn't abstract. It was personal and it was devastating.

Work didn't stop. But pretending nothing had happened wasn't an option.

We brought in grief counselors. We gave people time and space to process what had happened. We acknowledged the loss openly and honestly — in team meetings, in one on one conversations, in the way we adjusted expectations for the days that followed. We let people be human beings first and employees second for as long as they needed.

And we got through it together.

Most small business owners never think about grief as a continuity scenario. But when you build a real team — with real relationships and real culture — loss hits differently than it does in a transactional workplace. The closer the team, the deeper the impact.

Know this before it happens: your response in those moments will define your relationship with your team more than almost anything else you ever do. The owner who shows up with humanity and compassion when everything is hardest earns a loyalty that no compensation package can replicate.

What Human Continuity Looks Like in Practice

You can't script grief. You can't plan for every human crisis. But you can build the habits and relationships that make your team more resilient when the unthinkable happens.

Know your people. Not just their job performance — their lives. Their families. What matters to them. When something goes wrong, that knowledge is what allows you to respond with genuine care rather than generic protocol.

Have resources ready before you need them. Know who to call for employee assistance, grief counseling, or mental health support in your area. Having that information on hand means you can act quickly when someone needs help rather than scrambling to find it in the middle of a crisis.

Give people permission to be human. In a service business the pressure to keep operating is real and constant. But a team that feels seen and supported during the hardest moments will give you everything they have when it matters most. A team that feels like the business comes before their humanity will give you the minimum — and leave when something better comes along.

The freight train keeps moving. But the people running it are what make it go. Take care of them — especially when it's hardest.

You Can't Prepare for Everything — But Prepare Anyway

I wasn't prepared for COVID. Nobody was.

But the habits I had built before it hit — the team culture, the documented processes, the financial reserves, the operational discipline — made the difference between a business that bent and a business that would have broken.

You can't anticipate every crisis. You can't build a plan for every scenario. And honestly — if you tried, you'd spend so much time planning that you'd never have time to run the business.

What you can do is build a resilient operation — one with strong people, clear processes, secure facilities, appropriate insurance, and enough financial runway to absorb a shock without panicking. An operation where no single point of failure — no one person, no one system, no one vendor, no one customer — can bring the whole thing down.

The goal of continuity planning isn't to prevent disruption. It's to make sure that when disruption comes — and it will — you're still standing when it passes.

Build that business now. Before you need it.

Action Checklist:

- Identify your critical roles — who do you absolutely need besides yourself to keep operating?
- Document processes for every critical role so institutional knowledge isn't trapped in one person's head
- Cross-train backups for every critical function
- Build a pipeline — always be developing the next person for key roles
- Invest in culture — a solid team that pulls together is your most resilient continuity asset
- Know your software and technology vulnerabilities — identify backup providers before you need them
- Keep your data backed up and accessible independent of any single vendor
- Identify backup vendors for your most critical supplies and services
- Secure your facility position — get off month to month arrangements as soon as possible
- Build a weather and disruption protocol — who makes the call, how is it communicated, how do you reschedule
- Never put cost savings ahead of employee safety in a weather event
- Review your insurance coverage annually — general liability, commercial auto, workers comp, business interruption, umbrella, employment practices
- Maintain a cash reserve of two to three months of operating expenses
- Secure a line of credit while your financials are strong — before you need it
- Invoice immediately and collect receivables consistently — don't let them pile up
- Diversify your customer base — no single customer should represent a dangerous share of revenue
- Build strong vendor relationships through consistent payment and communication
- Know your people — their lives, their families, what matters to them

- Have employee assistance and grief counseling resources identified before you need them
- Give people permission to be human during difficult moments — productivity follows humanity
- Accept that you can't prepare for everything — build resilience instead of trying to predict every scenario
- Review your continuity plan annually — what has changed in your operation that creates new vulnerabilities?

PRINCIPLE 9: Build a Competition-Proof Business Through Consistent, Impeccable Service

Every good idea gets copied.

If you've built something worth having — a loyal customer base, a growing revenue stream, a reputation people trust — someone will notice. They'll study your model, duplicate what they can see, and enter your market with a lower price and a promise to do what you do for less.

This is not a threat to prepare for. It's a reality to build around.

The businesses that survive competition don't survive because they were first. They survive because they built something that can't be replicated by copying the concept. Culture can't be copied. Relationships can't be copied. A decade of operational refinement and a team that genuinely cares can't be copied. Those things have to be built — slowly, deliberately, one customer interaction at a time.

This principle is about building that kind of business. One that doesn't just withstand competition — but becomes stronger because of it.

The Bridge from Principle 7

In Principle 7 we talked about delivering superior value and earning the right to charge more. Everything in that principle feeds directly into this one.

The customer service organization philosophy. The delight versus satisfaction distinction. The investment in your team and your culture. The commitment to quality at every level of the operation.

Those aren't just retention tools. They're competitive weapons.

When a competitor enters your market — and they will — the customers who feel genuinely valued, consistently delighted, and completely confident in what you deliver are not going anywhere. They're not looking for alternatives because they've already found something worth keeping.

Build the loyalty before the competition arrives. By the time they show up, the customers worth having should already be yours.

What Corporate Taught Me About Competition

Early in my corporate career I worked in a telecommunications environment where competition was limited. Cable companies had exclusive franchise agreements with the towns they served. The market was protected. Complacency was easy.

Then broadband changed everything.

New technology allowed competitors to enter markets that had previously been closed. And when a major national competitor launched a comparable product — with significant marketing spend and an aggressive pricing strategy — my team was charged with one job: stop people from switching.

Here's the honest truth about what saved customers: rich discounts moved the needle more than anything else in the short term. That's reality. Price is a powerful retention tool and I won't pretend otherwise.

But here's what I observed over time. The customers who stayed because of a discount stayed until the discount expired — and then reconsidered again. The customers who stayed because of the relationship, the service experience, and the genuine sense that someone on our team cared about them — those customers stayed.

The telecommunications industry as a whole had earned a reputation for poor customer service — long hold times, missed appointments, billing errors, indifferent agents. It was a perception that followed the entire industry regardless of which provider a customer used. The bar was so low that basic human decency felt remarkable.

My company was actively working to be the exception to that reputation. And my team took that commitment further than anyone asked them to. Better training. Better tools. A genuine investment in treating every customer like their business mattered. When someone called to cancel and reached an agent who actually listened and actually tried — that experience alone was often enough.

We weren't just differentiating from the competitor. We were differentiating from an industry-wide expectation. And that gap — between what customers expected and what we actually delivered — was where loyalty was built.

You can't build a sustainable business on discounts. You can build one on relationships. The investment we made in our people — in their skills, their confidence, and their genuine care for the customer — minimized the impact of competition in a way that no pricing strategy ever could.

The lesson I carried into every business since: your team is the differentiating factor. Anyone can copy your product. Nobody can copy your culture.

Know Your Differentiators

Before you can protect what makes you competition-proof you have to be able to articulate it clearly.

Most owners have a general sense that they're better than their competitors — but struggle to say exactly why in a way that's specific and defensible. "We have better customer service" is not a differentiator. It's a claim. Every competitor makes the same claim.

A real differentiator is specific, provable, and meaningful to the customer.

Sit down and identify your top three. Not ten. Three. The things you do better than anyone else in your market that a customer can actually feel and verify. It might be your response time. Your error rate. Your team's tenure and consistency. Your reliability record. Your reviews relative to competitors. Your willingness to make things right when something goes wrong.

Once you know what they are — build every operational and marketing decision around protecting and amplifying those specific advantages. That's where your investment belongs. That's what your online presence should communicate. That's what your team should be trained to deliver consistently every single day.

Vague culture talk doesn't win customers. Specific, provable excellence does.

The Copycat Paradox

When I built my service business I was early to market. The concept was relatively new in my area and the early years felt like wide open territory.

Then the copycats appeared.

Other operators noticed what I was building and launched their own versions. Same basic concept. Lower prices. Aggressive marketing.

My first instinct was concern. My second was to watch what actually happened.

The competitors who copied my model didn't eat my market share. They grew the market.

Their advertising introduced the concept to people who didn't know it existed. They created awareness that my own marketing couldn't have generated alone. And when those newly aware customers did their homework — when they read reviews, compared reputations, and looked for the operator they could trust — they found me.

Copies generate awareness. Quality captures the customer.

The customers who chose a competitor based on price often discovered what that decision actually meant — in quality, in reliability, in the experience of dealing with an operation that hadn't built the culture and the systems to back up its promises.

Some of them came back.

The Grass Isn't Always Greener

One of my contract customers decided to switch to a lower cost provider. The person managing the account felt my pricing was too high and made the decision based on cost alone. The referrals that had been coming from that relationship stopped as they onboarded the new provider.

Three months later she called.

Their new provider was a mess. Complaints. Errors. Inconsistent service. Everything she had taken for granted when working with me had disappeared — and she was now managing the fallout.

She learned a valuable lesson that I've applied to every aspect of how I run my business: you get what you pay for.

Not just in the services you sell — but in everything you put into the operation. The employees you hire and what you pay them. The supplies and materials you use — quality name brands versus the cheapest option. The vendors and partners you choose. The systems you invest in.

Quality in. Quality out.

When you cut corners on inputs you eventually deliver a diminished output. Your customers notice — even if they can't always articulate exactly what changed. And when they finally experience a competitor who cut those same corners, they understand in a way they never could have before exactly what they had with you.

She came back. And she was more loyal than she had ever been — because now she knew.

Responding to the Price Objection

At some point a customer will tell you that a competitor charges less. How you respond in that moment matters enormously.

The wrong response is to immediately discount. That signals that your price was arbitrary to begin with and trains customers to negotiate every time.

The right response acknowledges the difference honestly and then redirects to value.

Something like: *"You're right that they charge less — and I respect that price matters. What I'd encourage you to consider is what you're actually comparing. Our error rate is X. Our reliability record is Y. Our reviews say Z. When something goes wrong — and in this business something occasionally does — here's how we handle it. I can't speak to what they do, but I can show you exactly what we do. Ultimately that decision is yours and I respect it either way."*

Then stop talking. Let the customer decide.

You're not arguing. You're not discounting. You're giving them the information they need to make a genuinely informed comparison — and trusting that the comparison works in your favor because you've built something worth the difference.

Customers who choose based on price alone were never your best customers. Customers who choose based on value — informed by evidence — become your most loyal ones.

Open the Door

Here's a philosophy that requires confidence to practice: when a customer leaves for a competitor, leave the door open for their return.

Not grudgingly. Not with conditions. With genuine warmth and no judgment.

Some customers have to learn the hard way. They're convinced the grass is greener somewhere else — that a lower price means the same value, that a newer operation has figured out something you haven't. Let them find out. Wishing them well costs you nothing and preserves the relationship for what comes next.

When they come back — and many will — welcome them like they never left. Don't make them feel foolish for leaving. Don't use their return as leverage. Just pick up where you left off and deliver the same excellent service that made them a customer in the first place.

A small gesture goes a long way. A handwritten note. A brief personal call. Something that says — we're glad you're back and we're going to remind you why you came back every single day.

The customer who left and returned is one of your most powerful promoters. They have a comparison now. They know what the alternative looks like. And when someone in their network asks for a recommendation — they don't just say you're good. They say they left, they learned, and they came back. That story is worth more than any five star review from a customer who never considered leaving.

The Proactive Win-Back

Don't just wait for customers to return on their own. Some of them need a nudge.

A customer who has gone quiet — whose activity has dropped, whose engagement has faded — is telling you something before they tell you they're leaving. Watch for those signals in your metrics dashboard. When you see them, reach out.

Not with a sales pitch. With genuine curiosity. A personal message or call that says — we've noticed we haven't heard from you lately and we wanted to check in. Is everything okay? Is there anything we can do better?

That conversation does two things simultaneously. It shows the customer they matter enough to be noticed. And it gives you information — either they're fine and just busy, or something happened that you have a chance to address before you lose them permanently.

A simple proactive win-back system — a quarterly review of customer activity, a personal outreach to anyone who has gone quiet, recovers customers who would otherwise drift away without ever telling you why.

Your Online Presence Is Competitive Armor

Most customers do their homework before they commit. They search. They read reviews. They compare options. They look for signals that tell them which operator they can trust.

When that moment happens — when a potential customer is evaluating you against a competitor — your online presence is either working for you or against you. There is no neutral.

Start with your Google Business Profile.

This is the single most important step for any local service business and it's completely free. Your Google Business Profile controls how you appear in local search results — your hours, your location, your reviews, your photos, your response to customer feedback. If you haven't claimed and optimized yours, do it today. It is the foundation of your local online presence and the first thing a potential customer will see when they search for what you offer.

From there — build a consistent presence on the platforms where your customers are. For most local service businesses that means Google reviews, Facebook, and whatever industry-specific platforms are relevant to your market.

Make customer reviews a system not an afterthought.

Reviews don't accumulate by accident. They require a consistent process — asking every satisfied customer at the right moment, making it easy with a direct link to your review profile, and following up gently if they expressed intention but didn't follow through.

The right moment to ask is immediately after a great experience — when the positive feeling is fresh and the customer is most motivated to share it. A simple message that says *"We're so glad you're happy with the service — if you have a moment to share your experience on Google it means the world to us and helps others find us"* with a direct link is all it takes.

Respond to every review. Positive ones deserve a genuine thank you that acknowledges something specific. Negative ones deserve a calm, professional response that acknowledges the experience and offers to make it right offline. Your response is as visible as the review itself — and how you handle criticism tells potential customers more about you than the criticism does.

The landscape is shifting faster than most owners realize.

A customer recently told me she found my business by asking an AI assistant who the best local service provider was in her area. We came up first.

It's not magic. It's the result of years of building a strong, consistent online presence — genuine reviews, an optimized Google Business Profile, an active and professional social media presence. The same signals that make you visible in traditional search are increasingly the signals that AI-powered search draws from.

The owners who invest in their online reputation today are not just preparing for how customers find businesses now. They're preparing for how customers will find businesses tomorrow.

The competitor who enters your market with a lower price but a thin online presence and sparse reviews is not your equal in the customer's eyes — regardless of what they charge. The customer who does their homework will find you first, trust you more, and choose you even if you cost more.

Build your online presence before the competition arrives. Every review you earn and every response you post is a brick in a wall that competitors have to climb.

Invest in What Makes You Different

Competition has a way of clarifying what actually matters in your business.

When a competitor enters your market you quickly discover which of your advantages are real and which were just the result of being the only option. The real advantages — the ones that hold up under competitive pressure — are almost always rooted in people, culture, and operational excellence rather than price or convenience.

Invest accordingly.

Pay your people well — and know what well means. Generous intentions aren't enough. Review your compensation against local market rates at least once a year. The team member who discovers they're being paid below market doesn't announce it — they start looking. Staying competitive on compensation is part of protecting the team that makes you competition-proof.

Beyond pay — invest in development. Compensation attracts people. Growth keeps them. Training, mentorship, clear career paths, and the genuine sense that they're getting better at their craft are what turn good employees into great ones and great ones into long-term assets. The team member who feels like they're growing is far less likely to leave than one who feels like they've plateaued regardless of what they earn.

Think deliberately about who you hire and what perspectives they bring. A team with varied backgrounds, experiences, and ways of connecting with people serves a broader range of customers more effectively. Different team members resonate with different customers. That breadth of connection is itself a competitive advantage.

Use quality materials and supplies. The difference in cost between a quality input and a cheap one is almost always smaller than the difference in output. Customers notice. Your team notices. And the cumulative effect of consistently choosing quality over cost shows up in your reputation over time.

Choose vendors and partners who reflect your standards. The people and companies you work with are an extension of your operation. Surround the business with partners who share your commitment to doing things right.

Build Switching Costs Into Your Service

Beyond culture and relationships — there are practical reasons that make your service genuinely hard to leave. Think about them deliberately and build more of them.

Integrated systems that customers rely on. Established routines that fit seamlessly into their lives. Staff relationships that feel personal and trusted. Accumulated history and preferences that a new provider would have to rebuild from scratch.

Every one of these is a switching cost — not in a manipulative sense, but in the genuine sense that your service has become woven into your customer's life in a way that's worth more than a price difference.

Look for ways to deepen that integration. The more your service fits naturally into how your customers live and work — the more friction there is in walking away. That friction protects you far more reliably than any contract ever could.

Is Your Culture Actually Strong?

Here's an honest question most owners avoid: how do you know your culture is as strong as you think it is?

Culture is only as reliable as your ability to measure it accurately. And that requires creating genuine channels for honest feedback — not just assuming everything is fine because nobody is complaining.

A few questions worth asking regularly:

Would your team recommend working here to a friend? If the honest answer is uncertain — something needs attention.

Would your customers recommend you without being asked? Your metrics dashboard should tell you. If it doesn't — build the measurement.

When something goes wrong internally — do people tell you? Or do they manage around it hoping you won't notice? The answer to that question tells you more about your culture than any survey.

Create safe, genuine channels for honest feedback. Anonymous surveys. Regular one on ones where people feel truly heard. An environment where delivering bad news to the owner is seen as helpful rather than risky.

The owners who think their culture is great because nobody complains often discover too late that nobody complained because they didn't feel safe doing so. Don't be that owner.

Protect the Moat

When your team is your competitive advantage — when the relationships, the knowledge, and the culture they carry are what makes you competition-proof — that asset deserves legal protection as well as operational investment.

It's worth having a conversation with an employment attorney about non-solicitation agreements — provisions that prevent departing employees from taking customers or recruiting colleagues to a competitor. Not because you expect betrayal from your team. But because protecting what you've built is part of building it responsibly.

This isn't about distrust. It's about acknowledging that the moat you've built has real value — and that value is worth protecting through every available means.

You Can't Copy Culture

Here's the competitive reality that keeps me confident in the face of any competitor.

They can copy the concept. They can buy the same equipment. They can hire from the same labor pool. They can set up the same scheduling and the same pricing structure.

What they cannot do is walk in on day one with a team that has been coached, developed, and invested in over years. They cannot manufacture the trust that has been built with thousands of customers through thousands of consistent positive experiences. They cannot replicate the culture — the shared values, the standards, the genuine pride in the work — that took years to build.

Culture is the moat. It's the competitive advantage that a well-funded copycat cannot buy and a cheap imitation cannot fake.

Build it deliberately. Protect it fiercely. And when competition arrives, as it always does, let your culture do the talking.

Action Checklist:

- Accept competition as inevitable — build around it rather than being surprised by it
- Identify your top three specific differentiators — make them concrete and provable not abstract
- Build every operational and marketing decision around protecting and amplifying those differentiators
- Invest in your team before competition arrives — they are your most defensible advantage
- Review compensation against local market rates annually — generous

intentions aren't enough

- Invest in team development — training, mentorship, career path visibility
- Build deliberately for breadth of perspective on your team — it serves a broader customer base
- Build customer loyalty through consistent excellence — not discounts or promotions
- Never compete on price alone — it is a race to the bottom with no winner
- Use the value selling framework when price objections arise — acknowledge, articulate the gap, let them decide
- Claim and optimize your Google Business Profile today if you haven't already
- Make reviews a system — ask consistently, make it easy, respond to every one
- Build your online presence before competition arrives — every review is a brick in the wall
- Invest in your online reputation today — it protects you in both traditional and AI-powered search
- Watch for customers going quiet — proactive win-back outreach recovers people before they leave permanently
- When customers leave for a competitor — leave the door open with genuine warmth
- Welcome returning customers without judgment — a small gesture goes a long way
- Apply "you get what you pay for" to everything — salaries, supplies, vendors, systems
- Build switching costs into your service — deepen integration into your customers' lives
- Create honest feedback channels — culture is only as strong as your ability to measure it accurately
- Consider non-solicitation agreements — protecting the moat has a legal dimension worth addressing
- Invest in your culture deliberately — shared values and standards are what competitors cannot copy

- Audit your competitive position annually — what are your real advantages and are you protecting them?
- Remember: anyone can copy your concept — nobody can copy your culture

PRINCIPLE 10: Turn It Off and Manage Worry — Reclaim Your Life Outside the Business

This principle is different from the others.

In every other principle I've shared what worked — the systems, the strategies, the lessons that moved the needle. I wrote them with confidence because I lived them and they proved out.

This one I'm still living. And I haven't figured it all out yet.

If you're reading this at midnight unable to sleep, your mind cycling through tomorrow's problems, your stomach already tightening at the thought of what the morning might bring — I don't want you to hear from someone who has it all figured out.

I want you to hear from someone who understands.

What It Actually Costs

Let me tell you what the road I took actually cost me.

I lost my credit. Years of borrowing personally to bridge business gaps, high debt ratios, hard inquiries — the financial foundation I should have been building for myself was being consumed by the business instead.

I lost my marriage. The business demanded everything — time, energy, presence, emotional bandwidth. There wasn't enough left for the relationship. That's a loss I carry.

I lost time I can't get back. Vacations I didn't take. Nights out I skipped. Moments with family and friends I was physically present for but mentally absent from because part of my brain was always back at the business.

And some days I lost pieces of my sanity — the constant mental load, the worry that never fully went away, the feeling that I was always one bad week away from a crisis even when things were going well.

I'm not telling you this to frighten you away from the journey. I'm telling you because I wish someone had told me — so I could have been smarter about the personal cost, minimized the damage where possible, and made more deliberate choices about what I was willing to sacrifice and what I wasn't.

Much of what I did, I did the hard way. I took the long road because shorter paths weren't visible. I wish I'd had this book when I first started. Not that it would have made a complete difference — some things you have to live through. But these lessons are something you can take and use. And if even one of them saves you from a cost I paid unnecessarily — then writing it was worth everything.

The Dream at 40

When I was 40 years old and still in the corporate trenches — good career, steady paycheck, no real freedom — I said something to myself that I've never forgotten.

I want to wake up each day and have work be optional.

Not retire. Not stop working. Just have the choice. Have time matter more than money for once — because at 40, working for someone else, time was the one thing I never had enough of.

That became the goal. Not a revenue number. Not a valuation. Not a title. Just that — work optional. Time mine. Freedom real.

Fifteen years later, at 55, I have it.

It didn't come free. You've read what it cost. But it came.

The Worry Doesn't Disappear

Here's what nobody tells you about reaching the goal: the worry doesn't fully go away.

Even now — with systems in place, a team that runs the operation without me, customers signing up, invoices processing — there is still a pit in my stomach most mornings.

The morning is when most problems surface. An employee issue. A customer complaint. A metric that moved the wrong way. The morning is when the business announces itself and demands your attention before you've had a chance to remember that you're not in the trenches anymore.

I've learned to sit with that feeling rather than fight it. To let it be there without letting it run the day. To check what needs to be checked, address what needs to be addressed, and then — deliberately, intentionally — close the laptop and step back into my life.

Not a skill I was born with. One I'm still developing.

You Are Not Alone — And This Is Not Weakness

Before we talk about what helps, I want to say something that I wish someone had said to me much earlier.

What you're feeling — the chronic background hum of worry, the sleepless nights, the inability to fully disconnect, the weight that follows you everywhere — is not a personal failure. It is a known occupational hazard of entrepreneurship.

Research consistently shows that business owners experience significantly higher rates of anxiety, stress, and burnout than the general population. Not because they are weaker. Because what they carry is genuinely heavier. The financial exposure is personal. The decisions are consequential. The responsibility for other people's livelihoods is real and it is constant.

Knowing that doesn't make the weight lighter. But it does mean you're not broken. You're human. And you're doing one of the hardest things a person can choose to do.

There is no weakness in acknowledging that. There is only wisdom.

The Business and the Person Are Not the Same Thing

Here is one of the deepest psychological challenges of entrepreneurship — and one of the least discussed.

When you build something from scratch, the line between who you are and what you built becomes dangerously blurred. Every business problem starts to feel like a personal failure. Every threat to the business feels like a threat to your identity. Every bad week feels like evidence that you were never really good enough to begin with.

That blurring is understandable. You poured yourself into this thing. Of course it feels like you.

But it isn't you. It's something you built. And those are very different things.

The business can have a hard month and you can still be a capable, worthy, accomplished person. The business can lose a customer and it doesn't mean you failed. The business can face a crisis and you can navigate it without it defining who you are.

Learning to separate your identity from your business is some of the most important inner work an owner can do. It doesn't happen overnight. It may require help from a therapist or a trusted mentor. But the owners who manage the mental load most effectively are almost always the ones who have done this work — who understand that they are not their business, and that their worth as a person is not determined by their revenue.

What Helps

Here are the tools that have actually helped me — not theory, not research, but what I reach for when the weight gets heavy.

Perspective. When the worry is loudest I make myself stop and look at how far I've come. I didn't just survive the early years — I built something. Something real, something valuable, something that runs without me. Most people who start a service business don't make it. I did. That reminder doesn't eliminate the worry but it puts it in its proper place.

Gratitude practiced deliberately. Not as a concept — as a daily habit. Before the phone comes out in the morning, write down three specific things that are genuinely good right now. Not vague positivity — specific, real things. The employee who has never let you down. The customer who renewed their contract. The morning that started without a crisis. The brain that is wired for threat detection needs to be consciously redirected toward what is working. It takes practice but it changes how the day begins.

Physical movement. Exercise is not optional when you're carrying the mental load of ownership. It's the most reliable reset available. A morning walk, a workout, time in nature — whatever form it takes for you, protect it like a business meeting. It changes the chemistry of the worry in a way that nothing else does. Move your body before you check your phone. The order matters.

A shutdown ritual. The brain needs a clear signal that work is done for the day — not just a gradual drift toward distraction. Build a deliberate end-of-day sequence that creates a psychological boundary between work mode and personal mode. It might be closing every tab and writing tomorrow's top three priorities. It might be a short walk. It might be a specific phrase you say out loud. Whatever it is — make it consistent. The ritual tells your nervous system that it's safe to let go for now. Without it, the business follows you everywhere.

Separating the urgent from the important. Most of what feels like an emergency at 6am is not an emergency by noon. Building the habit of sitting with a problem for an hour before reacting — rather than firing off responses the moment the anxiety peaks — saves enormous energy and usually produces better decisions. Ask yourself: does this need to be addressed in the next hour or the next day? Most of the time the answer is the next day.

Responsible technology boundaries. The phone is the umbilical cord between you and the business. It is also the thing that prevents you from ever truly leaving. Designate times when the phone is down — for dinner, for a conversation, for a morning walk. If you're worried about missing a genuine emergency, designate a backup contact who can reach you if something truly urgent arises. The business will not collapse in the time it takes to be present somewhere else. And your presence elsewhere — real, genuine presence — is what protects the relationships the business can't replace.

Talking to someone. A therapist, a trusted friend, a mentor, a peer who understands what this life actually feels like. The mental load of ownership is real and it is heavy and it is not something you should carry entirely alone. There is no weakness in asking for help carrying it. In fact the owners who ask for help earliest tend to carry it best.

Professional support when needed. Here's how to know when the worry has crossed from normal to something that needs attention: when it's affecting your sleep consistently, your physical health, your ability to make decisions, or your most important relationships — that's the signal. Not a bad week. Not a hard season. Persistent, pervasive, life-limiting anxiety deserves professional support. Talk to a doctor or a mental health professional. The tools available are genuinely effective and the stigma around using them is dissolving. You built something that required extraordinary resilience. Investing in your mental health is not a sign that the resilience ran out. It's a sign that you're smart enough to maintain the most important asset in the operation — yourself.

Faith and whatever grounds you. For many owners the thing that ultimately quiets the worry isn't a tactic or a tool — it's a deeper sense of meaning and trust. Whatever that looks like for you — a faith tradition, a philosophy, a connection to something larger than the business — lean into it. This principle looks different for everyone. The point is not the specific practice but the function it serves: something that reminds you that the business is not the whole of life, that your worth is not determined by your revenue, and that some things are simply outside your control and always will be. Find that anchor. Hold onto it.

Systems Are a Mental Health Strategy

Here's a connection I want to make explicit — because it changed how I thought about the work in Principles 3 and 4.

Every system you build reduces your mental load. Every process you document takes a decision out of your head and puts it on paper where it belongs. Every function you successfully delegate is weight you no longer have to carry personally.

The owner dependency problem isn't just a business efficiency problem. It's a mental health problem. When you are the only person who can make certain decisions, handle certain situations, or solve certain problems — the business never truly lets you go. It follows you to dinner. It wakes you up at 3am. It sits in the passenger seat on every vacation you try to take.

Building systems isn't just good for the business. It's good for you. Every hour you invest in Principle 4 is an hour invested in your own freedom and peace of mind.

Build the systems. Not just because the business needs them — because you do.

Have a Succession Plan

One of the quietest sources of owner anxiety is a question that rarely gets asked out loud: what happens to all of this if something happens to me?

If you were suddenly unable to run the business tomorrow — illness, accident, family emergency — what would happen? Who would make decisions? Who would communicate with customers and employees? Who would keep the freight train on the tracks?

Not having an answer to that question is itself a source of chronic low-level anxiety. It lives in the background even when everything is fine — the nagging awareness that the whole structure depends on your continued presence and health.

A basic succession plan doesn't have to be elaborate. It needs to answer a few key questions: who runs the business if I can't? What decisions do they have authority to make? Where are the critical documents, passwords, and contacts? How would customers and employees be informed?

Writing those answers down — even in a simple document — doesn't just protect the business. It quiets a worry you may not have even realized you were carrying.

Take Care of Your Team's Mental Load Too

The owner's mental health doesn't just affect the owner. It ripples through the entire organization.

An owner who is burned out, chronically anxious, or emotionally depleted creates instability that their team can feel — even when nothing is said out loud. Irritability, inconsistent decisions, emotional unavailability, reactive leadership — these things damage culture in ways that take years to repair.

Taking care of yourself is not separate from taking care of your business. It is part of it.

And consider your team's mental load as well. Small businesses can access employee assistance programs (confidential counseling and mental health support for employees), often at very low cost. If your team is carrying stress, pressure, or personal struggles that affect their work and their lives, having that resource available sends a clear message: we take care of people here. That message is part of your culture. And culture, as we've established, is your greatest competitive advantage.

Model the boundaries you want your team to have. If you respond to emails at midnight, your team feels obligated to do the same. If you never truly disconnect, the unspoken norm is that nobody should. The owner who models healthy boundaries — who visibly disconnects, who protects personal time, who demonstrates that the business can function without constant oversight — gives their team permission to do the same.

Lean Into Your Mentors

I was extraordinarily fortunate in my corporate career to be influenced by brilliant people — leaders who took the time to share what they knew, challenge how I thought, and point me toward paths I couldn't see on my own.

I made plenty of mistakes along the way. That never stopped. But I genuinely don't believe I could have built what I built — or become who I became — without the lessons and principles those people shared with me. I am forever grateful for them.

Find your mentors. Seek them out deliberately. Ask the questions you're afraid sound naive. Listen more than you talk. And when someone who has walked the road ahead of you offers to share what they learned — receive it with humility and use it with purpose.

The best mentors don't give you shortcuts. They give you perspective. They help you see around corners you didn't know were coming. They remind you — when the road is hard and the doubt is loud — that others have been exactly where you are and found their way through.

If you don't have an obvious mentor in your life — look for one deliberately. Local business associations, industry groups, SCORE (a free mentoring resource available to small business owners across the country) — LinkedIn connections, former employers, peers who are a few steps ahead of you on the road. The mentor you need is often closer than you think. But they rarely appear without being sought.

And one day, when you've built something worth building and learned something worth sharing — pay it forward. Be the mentor someone else needed. Pass the lessons on.

That's what this book is. My attempt to be — for you — what those brilliant people were for me.

The Summer Office

I want to tell you what work optional actually looks like for me now. Because I think you deserve to see the destination — not just the road.

I wake up in the morning — still not fully accustomed to the freedom, even now — and I open my windows and breathe in the fresh morning air. I exercise. If there's something work-related that needs my attention I handle it. If there isn't — I'm free. Free to start new projects. Free to visit family and friends. Free to focus on whatever I find meaningful or enjoyable that day.

And in the summer I have what I call my office — my pool.

I'll be out there on a Tuesday afternoon, the sun on my face, the day entirely mine — and I'll glance at my phone and see new customer signups coming in. Invoices being processed. The business doing what it was built to do, without me having to be in the building for it to happen.

In those moments the worry goes quiet.

Not because nothing could go wrong. But because I remember — in a way that's physical, not just intellectual — exactly why I did this. Exactly what these long years of sacrifice and perseverance and hard mornings and sleepless nights was building toward.

This.

A Tuesday afternoon in the pool with nowhere I have to be.

And in the winter, my office moves too. Sometimes it's somewhere tropical. Sometimes it's a cruise ship. Not when I'm past retirement age and too tired to enjoy it — now, while I'm still young enough to feel it. Not someday. Now.

That's work optional. That's time mattering more than money. That's the exit from the corporate trenches that a 40-year-old made a promise to himself about — and kept.

You can build this too. Not identically — your version will look different from mine. But the freedom is real and it is achievable and it is worth every hard thing you will go through to get there.

The Long Road Was Worth It

I took the hard road. I paid costs I didn't have to pay because I didn't have the map. I made mistakes that cost me money, relationships, and years I can't recover.

But I also built something from nothing. Scaled it past a million dollars. Created jobs for people who needed them. Delivered a service that genuinely improved people's lives. Built a team that operates without me. Earned a reputation strong enough to show up first when someone asks an AI who the best provider is.

And I wrote this book — so that maybe, just maybe, your road is a little shorter than mine. A little less costly. A little more deliberate.

You're going to have hard mornings. You're going to feel the knot in your stomach. You're going to wonder at some point whether it's worth it.

It is.

Keep going.

Action Checklist:

- Define what work optional means to you — make it specific and write it down
- Acknowledge the personal costs of ownership honestly — know what you're willing to sacrifice and what you're not
- Understand that chronic worry is a known occupational hazard of entrepreneurship — not weakness
- Do the work of separating your identity from your business — you are not your revenue
- Build the business to run without you from day one — owner dependency is a mental health problem as much as a business problem
- Practice perspective deliberately — regularly remind yourself how far you've come
- Build a daily gratitude habit — three specific things every morning before the phone comes out
- Protect physical movement — exercise before you check your phone and protect it like a meeting
- Build a shutdown ritual — a deliberate end-of-day sequence that signals work is done
- Separate urgent from important — sit with problems for an hour before reacting

- Set technology boundaries responsibly — designate a backup contact so you can truly disconnect
- Find your mentors — look in business associations, industry groups, SCORE, and your existing network
- Receive wisdom with humility and use it with purpose
- Build a support network — a peer, a mentor, someone who understands this life
- Know when to seek professional support — persistent anxiety that affects sleep, health, and relationships deserves attention
- Lean into whatever grounds you — faith, meaning, purpose beyond the business
- Write a basic succession plan — answering the existential question reduces the anxiety that comes with it
- Model healthy boundaries for your team — you have to disconnect first
- Look into employee assistance programs for your team — mental health support is affordable and culturally powerful
- Pay it forward — when you've built something worth building, share what you learned
- Define your summer office — the place and the moment that reminds you why you did this
- When the worry is loudest — look at what the business is doing without you and remember
- Keep going — the freedom is real and it is worth the road it takes to get there

If you made it this far, thank you.

Writing this book was its own kind of trench — early mornings, late nights, and more than a few moments of wondering whether any of it was worth putting down on paper. I hope it was worth your time to read.

I didn't write this to impress anyone. I wrote it because I wish someone had handed me these pages twenty years ago. If even one principle saves you from a cost I paid unnecessarily — in money, in stress, or in lost time with the people who matter — then this book did its job.

I'd be grateful if you'd take two minutes to leave a review on Amazon. Reviews are the lifeblood of a book like this. They help other small business owners find it, and they tell me whether this conversation is worth continuing.

Leave a review: Search *Lessons from the Trenches* on Amazon

Visit: Trenchesbook.com
Reach out: scott@trenchesbook.com
You're building something. Keep going.
— Scott Waterman *U.S. Army National Guard Veteran*
Coventry, Rhode Island

ABOUT THE AUTHOR

Scott Waterman is a service business operator, entrepreneur, and U.S. Army National Guard Veteran with more than three decades of hands-on experience building, leading, and scaling operations.

He began his corporate career in 1998 as an inbound sales representative at a Fortune 500 telecommunications company, eventually rising to Director of Customer Retention for the Northeast Region — leading teams responsible for retaining millions of dollars in recurring revenue.

In 2011, Scott made the leap into entrepreneurship. He acquired, turned around, and profitably sold a small retail service business. He then founded a separate tech-enabled home delivery service in 2016, scaling it to over $1.2 million in annual revenue while building it into a largely owner-independent operation.

Scott served in the Military Police with the U.S. Army National Guard during the 1990s — an experience that shaped his belief in discipline, systems, and leading from the front.

He holds a Bachelor of Arts in Sociology with a Minor in Justice Studies from Rhode Island College.

Scott writes and consults on leadership, coaching, and the practical principles of building small businesses that run well, scale cleanly, and are worth something when it's time to walk away.

Visit: Trenchesbook.com

www.ingramcontent.com/pod-product-compliance
Lightning Source LLC
LaVergne TN
LVHW090533110826
845146LV00003B/1079

* 9 7 9 8 9 9 5 9 5 8 3 0 7 *